Basics of Statistics and SPSS

Seyed Reza Hashemian Rahaghi

Assisted by

Farnaz Abed Ashtiani

ISBN-13: 978-1461119531
ISBN-10: 1461119537

To

My Parents

Contents   Page

What is statistics?
Different Types of Statistics
      a. Descriptive Statistics
      b. Inferential Statistics
Descriptive Statistics
      a. Measurement Of central Tendency
          a.1: Mean
          a.2: Median
          a.3: Mode
          Example 1-1
      b. Measurement of Dispersion
          b.1: variance
          b.2: Standard deviation
      c. Measure of Skewness
      d. Measure of Kurtosis
Variable
      Different types of Variables
      a. Independent Variable
      b. Dependent Variable
      c. Mediating variable
      d. Moderating Variable
      e. Control variable
      Measurement level of Variables
      a. Metric
          a.1: Interval
          a2: Ratio
      b. Non-Metric
          b.1: Nominal
          b.2: Ordinal
      Variables and Statistical Tools
Bonus Points
Population

ACKNOWLEDGMENTS

Dear reader,

Quantitative part of research is emphasized by this book and qualitative side is not investigated widely. This book is suitable for who are going to do research and especially for Master of Science students that are out of any knowledge about SPSS. However, having basic computer knowledge is an obligation. Questions are hired in each chapter for introducing clearer understanding of the dilemma and our aim compulsorily is not finding the exact answers for all questions given in different chapters. The name and version of program which is hired in this book is SPSS17 respectively. An overview regarding different stages of doing a research such as sampling and testing the gotten data via SPSS is mentioned during the chapters.

Professor Dr. Murali Sambasivan's effort is appreciated and I offer my special gratitude to Ms. Ashtiani and Ms. Hashemian regarding their assistance. Furthermore, special thanks to Neville from Coventry University and Dr, William M. Trochim for giving me permission to hire the materials of their websites for improving the content of this book.

Best Regards

Seyed Reza Hashemian Rahaghi
E-mail: s.reza.hashemian@gmail.com

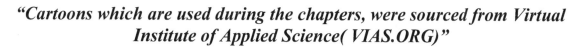

"Cartoons which are used during the chapters, were sourced from Virtual Institute of Applied Science(VIAS.ORG)"

(1998-G.Meixner)

"Pictures which are used for designing the cover, were sourced from www.stockphotopro.com"

Chapter 1: An Introduction to Statistics

What is Statistics?

Definition: Statistics is a science dealing with:
- Identification of Data
- Collection of Data
- Analysis of Data (According to the nature of variables we choose the analysis tool)
- Interpretation of Results
- Prepare a report explaining the results to the users / audiences

In a nut shell, statistic is data management and is used for converting information to data.

Different types of statistics:

a. Descriptive statistics:

This kind of statistics gives us a feel about the data in form of numbers, graphs .In other words, It describes the characteristics of a data set which can be in the form of numbers ,graphs, etc. e.g.: Mean, Standard Deviation, Correlation.
- Descriptive statistics associated with population is called parameters.
- Descriptive statistics associated with sample is called sample statistics.

b. Inferential statistic:

In this kind of statistics, we are involved with prediction. It is making inferences about the characteristics of a population based on information contained in the sample. In other words, it is making inference about population parameters based on sample statistic.

Descriptive statistics:

a. Measurement of central tendency:

It gives the central value of data set.

a.1: Mean:

For a <u>data set</u>, mean is the sum of the values divided by the number of values. The mean of a set of numbers $x_1, x_2... x_n$ is typically denoted by $\bar{X}$, pronounced "x bar".

$$\bar{X} = \frac{1}{n}\sum_{i=1}^{n} x_i$$

NOTICE: Usually, mean does not give correct result. Thus, we use median.

a.2: Median:

e.g.: If CGPA of a student was high ,it would be considered which he is a good student and it would not be important that how much he got in each subject.

a.3: Mode:

e.g.: In some tea factories, the duty of a few workers is testing the taste of tea .If most of them said which the taste is good, tea would be accepted.

Example 1-1:

Find the mean, median, mode, and range for the following list of values:

14, 19, 14,15,14,17,15,22,14

The mean is the usual average,

(14+19+14+15+14+17+15+22+14)/ 9=16

The median is the middle value. First, the numbers must be written in order.

14, 14, 14,14,15,15,17,19,22

Secondly, the following formula is used.

(n+1)÷2

While n shows the number of values.

$(9 + 1) \div 2 = 10 \div 2 = 5$

So, the median will be 5th number. (15)

The mode is the most repeated number. Thus, 14 is mode.

However, following the processes which were mentioned above can be so tiresome. Especially, when we are involved with a lot of numbers it can be more exhausting.

Some software can be used for getting the mean, median, mode. For instance with entering the values in Excel and hiring the related commands, results are gotten easily.

Related commands are as follows.

=average (selected values)

=median (selected values)

=mode (selected values)

C	D	E	F	G
14		Average	16	
14		Median	15	
14		Mode	14	
14				
15				
15				
17				
19				
22				

fx =AVERAGE(C1:C9)

Figure 1

For getting the range the smallest number is subtracted from the biggest number.
22-14=8
Notice that the values can be arranged in order with sort button which is located in Excel easily.

b. *Measure of dispersion:*
Dispersion shows how the data set is distributed around the mean.

b.1: *Variance:*

1 -G.Mixner 1998

A commonly used measure of dispersion is the **standard deviation**, which is simply the square root of the **variance**. The variance is one of indicators of variability that is hired to characterize the dispersion among the measures in a given population. For calculating the variance of a population, first calculate the mean of the values. Next, measure the amount that each value deviates from the mean and then square that deviation. Numerically, the variance equals the average of the several squared deviations from the mean.
The least amount of variance is zero and it cannot be negative. If it was negative, the number would be imaginary.

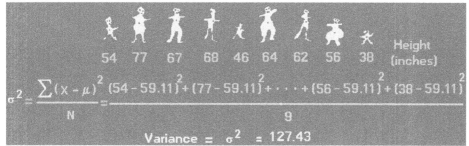

www.animatedsoftware.com

Formulas for calculating the variance of population and sample are as follows.

Variance of population $\sigma^2 = \frac{\sum_{i=1}^{n}(X_i-\mu)^2}{n}$

Variance of sample $\delta^2 = \frac{\sum_{i=1}^{n}(X_i-\overline{X})^2}{n-1}$

While σ^2 shows the population variance and σ indicates the standard deviation of population, the variance of sample is shown with δ^2. Furthermore, μ stands for mean of population and the sample mean is illustrated with $\overline{X}$.

While sample mean is an unbiased estimator of the population mean, the same is not true for the sample variance if it is calculated in the same manner as the population variance. Furthermore, if you take all possible samples of n members and calculated the sample variance of each combination using n in the denominator and averaged the results, the value would not be equal to the true value of the population variance; that is, it would be biased. However, with replacing the n with (n-1) in the denominator the bias can be corrected and the sample variance comes an unbiased estimator of the population variance. [3].

*NOTICE: Sometimes characters which are used in formulas are different in various books.

b.2: Standard deviation:

The standard deviation σ of a probability distribution is defined as the square root of the variance σ^2, s.d=$\sqrt{variance}$

c. Measure of Skewness:

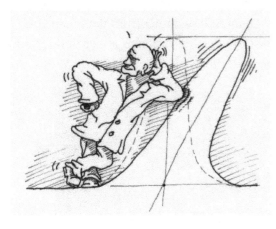

2 -G.Mixner 1998

It describes asymmetry from the normal distribution in a set of statistical data. If the left tail (tail at small end of the distribution) is more pronounced than or fatter than the right tail (tail at the large end of the distribution), the function is said to have negative skewness. If the reverse is true, it has positive skewness. If the two are equal, it has zero skewness.

As it can be evoked from illustration the skeweness of data set in symmetric or bell shaped is zero. Skewness describes asymmetry from the normal distribution in a set of statistical data. Skewness can come in the form of "negative skewness" or "positive skewness", depending on whether data points are skewed to the left (negative skew) or to the right (positive skew) of the data average. Skewness is extremely important in finance and investment. Most sets of data, including stock prices and asset returns, have either positive or negative skew rather than following the balanced normal distribution (which has a skewness of zero).By knowing which way data is skewed, one can better estimate whether a given (or future) data point will be more or less than the mean. Most advanced

Symmetric
Bell shaped

Skewed to
the Left

Skewed to
the Right

economic analysis models study data for skewness and incorporate this into their calculations. Skewness risk is the risk that a model assumes a normal distribution of data when in fact data is skewed to the left or right of the mean. [6].

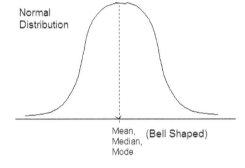

If there are extreme values towards the positive end of a distribution, the distribution is said to be **positively skewed**. In a positively skewed distribution, the mean is greater than the mode. For example :(See the next graph)

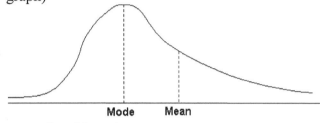

www.mathsrevision.net

Negative skew: The left tail is longer; the mass of the distribution is concentrated on the right of the figure. It has relatively few low values. The distribution is said to be left-skewed or "skewed to the left". Example (observations): 7, 3000,3001,3002,3003

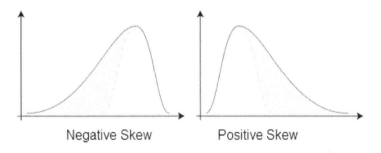

Von Hippel,Paul T

Positive skew: The right tail is longer; the mass of the distribution is concentrated on the left of the figure. It has relatively few high values. The distribution is said to be right-skewed or "skewed to the right". Example (observations): 5,6,7,8,200.

If the distribution is symmetric then the mean = median and there is zero skewness. (If, in addition, the distribution is unimodal, then the mean = median = mode.) This is the case of a coin toss or the series 1,2,3,4... [4], [5].

Formula for calculating the Skewness is as follows.

Skewness= $n \sum z^3 / [(n-1)(n-2)]$

Where z is calculated from the following equation,

$Z= (X_i-\mu) / \sigma$

While n is the number of observations and σ is standard deviation.

Skewness of Normal distribution is zero.
If number is bigger than zero, it is right skewness and vice versa.

d. Measure of kurtosis:

In measure of kurtosis, the Peakness of the data distribution is investigated .It could be narrow or flat or between them.In probability theory and statistics, **kurtosis** (from the Greek word

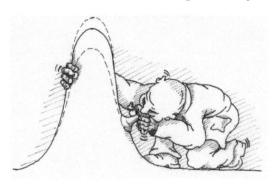

κυρτός, *kyrtos* or *kurtos*, meaning bulging) is a measure of the "peakedness" of the probability distribution of a real-valued random variable, although some sources are insistent that heavy tails, and not peakedness, is what is really being measured by kurtosis.

Higher kurtosis means more of the variance is the result of infrequent extreme deviations, as opposed to frequent modestly sized deviations. [10].

3 -G.Mixner 1998

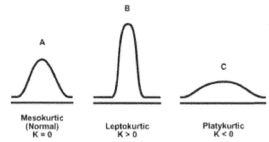

Kurtosis is calculated from equation below.

Kurtosis$=\{n(n+1)\sum z^4 /[(n-1)(n-2)(n-3)]\} - \{3(n-1)^2/[(n-2)(n-3)]\}$

More flat-top distribution ➜ value < 0, platykurtic
Less flat-top distribution ➜ value > 0, leptokurtic
Equally flat-top distribution ➜ value = 0, mesokurtic

Variable:

Definition: It is the fundamental building block in a quantitative research .Furthermore; it is characteristic which is measured.

Different types of variables:
a .Independent variable:
b. Dependent variable:

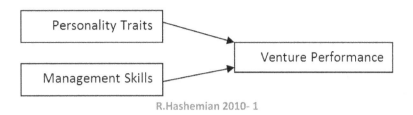

R.Hashemian 2010- 1

While Personality traits and management skills are determinants of the venture performance and they are called independent variables, the venture performance is called dependent variable .Since; venture performance depends on personality traits and management skill.

c. *Mediating variable:*

In illustration below, Variable M is a mediator of the relationship between T and O if M helps explain **how** or **why** T is related to O.

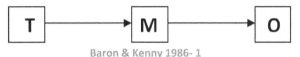

Baron & Kenny 1986- 1

In example below, venture performance is not directly affected by personality traits and opportunity recognition skills plays a role as a mediator.

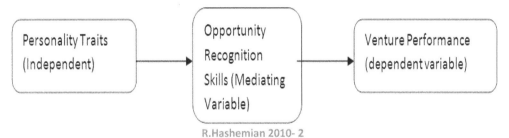

R.Hashemian 2010- 2

d. *Moderating variable:*

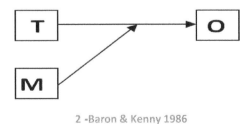

This variable plays an important role in financial issues. As it is seen from picture, Variable M is a moderator of the relationship between a target variable T and an outcome O in a particular population, if M explains for **whom** or **under what conditions** T is related to O.

2 -Baron & Kenny 1986

If in mentioned example we ignore the role of spouse support, the effect of independent variable on dependent variable would be completely different from the time which the mentioned role exists. In fact the relationship between independent and dependent variables is affected by the degree of spouse support.

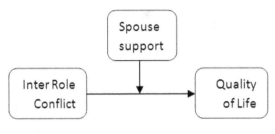

3 -R.Hashemian 2010

In some cases, categories play roles as moderators.eg: Mankind is divided in two categories according to sexuality (Gender).

It goes without any saying that amount of stress in people is affected by their sexuality.

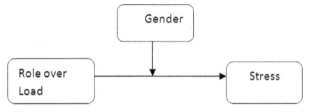

R.Hashemian 2010- 4

e. Control variable:

This variable plays an important role in social sciences.eg: size of the firm, type of the industry, etc.As it can be seen from the illustration below, the size of the company effects the information and accounting system of the firm .In brief, the whole frame work is affected by control variable.

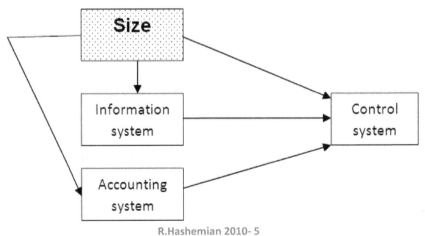

R.Hashemian 2010- 5

In addition of variable types which were mentioned above, **Manifest variable** and **Construct variable** are the common used terms in recent studies. Manifest variable is defined as the variable that is observed and measured. However, construct variable is an imaginary variable that is developed for the purpose of research and it is made of several manifest variables. In some articles the construct variable is called latent or hidden variable (latent or hidden construct). For instance, for measuring language skill, we have to evaluate some observable and measurable variables and without evaluating those variables, language skill would not be measured.

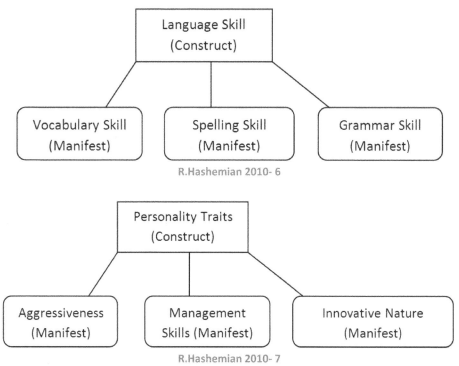

Measurement levels of variables:

a. Metric:
Definition: **Parametric Statistics** is statistical procedures that use interval-scaled or ratio-scaled data and assume population or sampling distribution with normal distributions.

a.1: Interval:
This group doesn't have absolute zero.

a.2: Ratio:
This group has absolute zero.

b. Non- metric:

Definition: **Nonparametric Statistics** is statistical procedures that use nominal or ordinal scaled data and make no assumptions about the distribution of the population (or sampling distribution).

b.1: Nominal:

In this group, data is in categories and cannot be ranked.eg:

Gender:-Male-Female (in the nature of creation, we cannot say male is better than female or vice versa)

Race:-Malay-Chinese-Indian-

b.2: Ordinal:

In this group, data is in categories and can be ranked. (Less than or more than).e.g.: Education level, Income level, Likert Scale.

*NOTICE:A **Likert scale** is a psychometric scale commonly used in questionnaires, and is the most widely used scale in survey research, such that the term is often used interchangeably with rating scale even though the two are not synonymous.[8]. When responding to a Likert questionnaire item, respondents specify their level of agreement to a statement. The scale is named after its inventor, psychologist Rensis Likert. [7].Furthermore, Measuring behavior, attitude....are kinds of likert scale.

*NOTICE: Nominal and ordinal are also called categorical variables. Since, they always are categorized.

		Categorized	Ranked	Distance	Real Zero	Example
Measurement Levels	Nominal	❖				Male/Female
	Ordinal	❖	❖			Ranking
	Interval	❖	❖	❖		Assessment of Beliefs
	Ratio	❖	❖	❖	❖	Weight

For better understanding the level of measurement, it is shown by an example as follows. This example has been sourced from **WWW.SOCIALRESEARCHMETHODS.NET.** In example below, party affiliation is a variable and it has some attributes.

Suppose in this election context the related attributes are "republican", "democrat", and

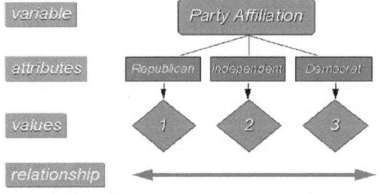

"independent". Regarding analyzing the results of this variable, 1, 2 and 3 are specified to three attributes (Republican, Independent, Democrat) respectively. The relationship among 1, 2, 3(three values) are described by level of measurement. In this example values are hired for simplifying the long text to short numbers and it doesn't mean that higher values or lower values indicate more or less than something respectively. We don't assume the value of 2 means that independents are twice something that republicans are. It is not supposed which democrats are in third place or republicans have the priority and are in first place. In this case, we only use the values as brief symbols for the attributes. Here, we would describe the level of measurement as "nominal".

Why is Level of Measurement Important?

Interpretation of the data from the particular variable is facilitated by knowing the level of measurement. When you know that a measure is nominal, then you know that the numerical values are just short codes for the longer names. Next, knowing the level of measurement plays a crucial role in recognition of the most suitable statistical tool and test on the related value. If a measure is nominal, then you know that you would never average the data values or do a t-test on the data.

Four levels of measurements are,

- Nominal
- Ordinal
- Interval
- Ratio

In **nominal** measurement the numerical values just "name" the attribute uniquely. No ordering of the cases is implied. For example, the numbers of players in basketball are measured at the nominal level. A player with number 25 is not more of anything than a player with number 14.

Contrary to nominal measurement, in **ordinal** measurement the attributes can be rank-ordered. However, distances between attributes do not have any meaning. Measuring the consumer satisfaction regarding the quality of a product is an example of ordinal measurement. Researcher may ask consumers to show their ideas as, very dissatisfied, somewhat dissatisfied, somewhat satisfied or very satisfied. As it is seen the items are ordered from the least satisfied to the most satisfied. Furthermore, on a survey you might code Educational Attainment as 0=less than H.S.; 1=some H.S.; 2=H.S. degree; 3=some college; 4=college degree; 5=post college. In this example, greater numbers mean *more* education. However, the distance between 0 and 1 is not same as 3 and 4. The **interval** between values is not interpretable in an ordinal measure.

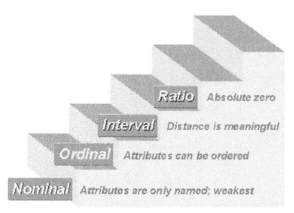

In **interval** measurement the distances between attributes have meaning. For example, when we measure temperature (in Fahrenheit), the distance from 20-30 is same as distance from 50-60. The interval between values is interpretable. Because of this, it makes sense to compute an average of an interval variable, where it doesn't make sense to do so for ordinal scales. But note that in interval measurement ratios don't make any sense - 90 degrees is not twice as hot as 45 degrees (although the attribute value is twice as large).Finally, in **ratio** measurement there is always an absolute zero that is meaningful. This means that you can construct a meaningful fraction (or ratio) with a ratio variable. Weight is a ratio variable. In applied social research most "count" variables are ratio, for example, the number of clients in past six months. Why? Because you can have zero clients and because it is meaningful to say that "...we had twice as many clients in the past six months as we did in the previous six months."It's important to recognize that there is a hierarchy implied in the level of measurement idea. At lower levels of measurement, assumptions tend to be less restrictive and data analyses tend to be less sensitive. At each level up the hierarchy, the current level includes all of the qualities of the one below it and adds something new. In general, it is desirable to have a higher level of measurement (e.g., interval or ratio) rather than a lower one (nominal or ordinal)."[9].

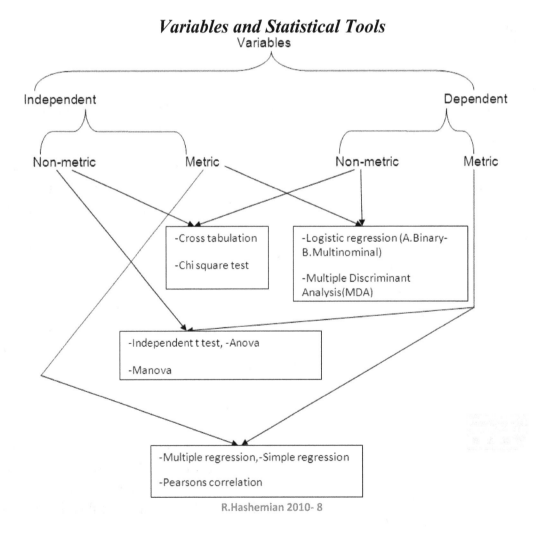

Variables and Statistical Tools

*NOTICE: Multiple regression usually is used in situation which dependent variables are the combination of metric and non-metric.

Bonus Points:

The most of the papers and articles follow the format below.

1) Introduction

-Brief background

-Motivation

-scope

-Contribution

-Organization of the paper

2) Theoretical framework and hypothesis development

3) Methodology section (what kind of technique you are going to use and why)

-population

-Sampling frame

-Unit of analysis

-Sampling strategy

-Instrument. Such as, questionnaire

-Measures….measurement of constructs

-Statistical tools

4) Results

-Descriptive statistics

-Inferential statistics

5) Discussion

-Theoretical implications

-Managerial implications

6) conclusions/limitations/directions for future research

Chapter 2: Different Sampling Methods

4 -G.Mixner 1998

Population:

Definition: It is defined as all elements of interest.

Sample: Definition: It is a small portion of population. Sample must have the characteristics of population. If the sample is not representative of the population, the result is not generalized to the population.

Selecting Sample Size:

One of the current issues in sampling is the size of samples which should be taken for different kinds of studies. Before starting to the process of sampling, some crucial issues must be considered precisely as follows,

- How much information was gotten from previous studies and is known to us.
- What are the parameters we would like to estimate?
- How much is the value of the research for us and how much time and cost we have to spend for sampling? If the test is so important, the risk value must be less. Thus, we have to spend more time and money.
- Notice that if monotonousness of population is less (variability is more); we have to get more samples.

For getting the most accurate sample size, different methods exist. Such as,

- There are different websites and companies which prepare the most accurate sample sizes and statistics tools for researchers who are not familiar with these issues.
- One of the best ways and especially for small populations is census or study the entire population.
- Another way is referring to studies which were done before and using the same procedures and sample sizes. Furthermore, reviewing the previous research in literature part of study and accepting the possible errors which is involved with that research is inevitable.
- One of the easy as well as precise strategies is hiring some software such as PASS. With entering the related values, the best estimation of sample size is generated.

The following example shows the processes which PASS is hired for obtaining sample size regarding the estimation of average an object in population based on CI (Confidence Interval).

Example1-2:

We would like to estimate average of monthly income among 2000 families in a small city. According to the primary information standard deviation is 380$ and CI equals to 95%.The amount of accepted error is 20$.

For getting the sample size the process below is followed.

Means ⇨ One Mean ⇨Confidence Intervals

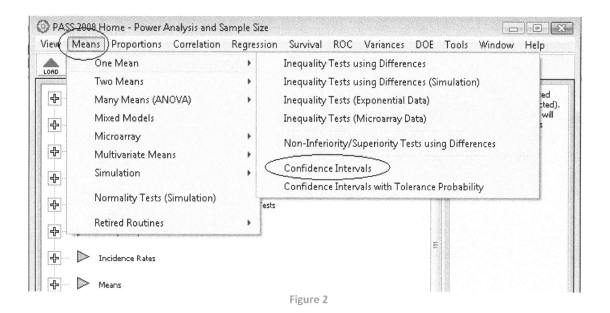

Figure 2

In revealed window information is entered and click on run button.

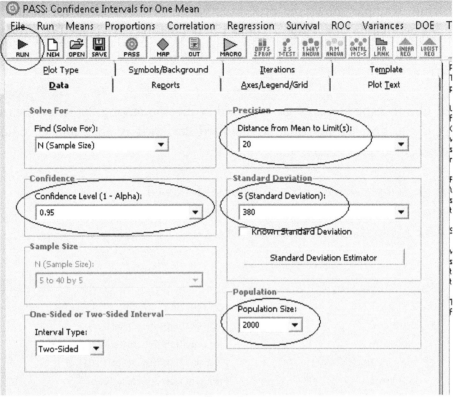

Figure 3

In illustration below the output is shown.

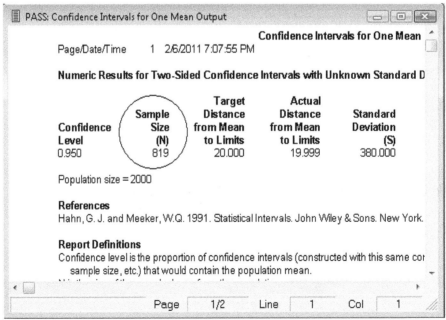

Figure 4

So, the minimum sample size is 819 families. Notice that this example is only a glance of PASS and widely investigating of this program is out of the main purpose of this book.

- The most convenient way for estimating the sample size is using the tables. This method usually is used in studies which their samples sizes are finite and almost small.(See tables 1,2,3 at the end of book)
- The last way for finding the sample size is using formulas. Regarding the type of study and size of population different equations are hired. Some of these formulas are as below.

Following formulas were sourced from website belong to University of Florida and the related document is from Glenn D.Israel(2009).

"Formula for Calculating a Sample for Proportions:

Formula for Calculating Samples For populations that are large (developed by Cochran):

$$n = \frac{Z^2 pq}{e^2}$$

n is the sample size, Z^2 is the abscissa of the normal curve that cuts off an area at the tails (1 - equals the desired confidence level, e.g., 95%), e is the desired level of precision(e.g. , 5%), p is the estimated proportion of an attribute that is present in the population, and q is 1-p. The value for Z is found in statistical tables which contain the area under the normal curve (e.g, 1.96) (See table 4 in Appendix).

For example we would like to investigate a province-wide program in which women are motivated to adopt family planning program. There is a large population and we do not know the variability in the proportion that will adopt the program; so, p=.5 (maximum variability). Furthermore, suppose we desire a 95% confidence level and ±5% precision.

$$\frac{(1.96)^2 * (0.5)(0.5)}{(0.05)^2} = 385 \; women$$

If the population is small then the sample size can be reduced slightly. So, equation comes as follows,

$$n = \frac{n_0}{1 + \frac{(n_0 - 1)}{N}}$$

Where n is the sample size and N is the population size. Suppose our evaluation of women' adoption of the program only affected 2,000 ones.

$$n = \frac{385}{1 + \frac{(385 - 1)}{2000}} = 323 \; women$$

This adjustment (called the finite population correction) can substantially reduce the necessary sample size for small populations.

Yamane (1967:886) provides a simplified formula to calculate sample sizes. This formula was used to calculate the sample sizes in Tables 1 and 2(See the appendix) and is shown below. A 95% confidence level and P =0 .5 are assumed for Equation below.

$$n = \frac{N}{1+N(e)^2} \quad , \quad n = \frac{2000}{1+2000(0.05)^2} = 333 \; women$$

Where n is the sample size, N is the population size, and e is the level of precision.

Formula for Sample Size for the Mean

$$n_0 = \frac{z^2 \sigma^2}{e^2}$$

Where n_0 is the sample size, z is the abscissa of the normal curve that cuts off an area at the tails, e is the desired level of precision (in the same unit of measure as the variance), and σ^2 is the variance of an attribute in the population.

The disadvantage of the sample size based on the mean is that a "good" estimate of the population variance is necessary. Often, an estimate is not available. Furthermore, the sample size can vary widely from one attribute to another because each is likely to have a different variance. Because of these problems, the sample size for the proportion is frequently preferred."[1].

Furthermore equations below can be used for estimation of sampling size too.

For more information regarding the following formulas refer to DETERMINING *SAMPLE SIZE FOR RESEARCH ACTIVITIES BY ROBERT V.KREJCIE AND DARYLE W.MORGAN.*

"s = X 2NP (1− P) ÷ d 2 (N −1) + X 2P (1− P).

s = required sample size.

X2 = the table value of chi-square for 1 degree of freedom at the desired confidence level (3.841).

N = the population size.

P = the population proportion (assumed to be .50 since this would provide the maximum Sample size)., d = the degree of accuracy expressed as a proportion (.05).

Or

"When Population size is unknown: $Sample \; size = \dfrac{(\frac{Range}{2})^2}{(\frac{accuracy \; Level}{Confidence \; level})^2}$

Accuracy levels: Range ×Desired level of accuracy (expressed as a proportion)

Confidence Levels		
Confidence levels	$\propto$	$\propto/2$
0.10	1.28	1.64
0.05	1.64	1.96
0.01	2.33	2.58
0.001	3.09	3.29

When Population size is known:$Size = \frac{X^2 NP(1-p)}{d^2(N-1)+X^2 P(1-p)}$

X^2=table value of chi-square @ df=1 for desired confidence level
0.10=2.71, 0.05=3.84, 0.01=6.64, 0.001=10.83
N=population size
P=population Proportion (assumed to be 0.50)
D=degree of accuracy (expressed as a proportion)". [2].
Note that,

- "In complex sampling methods, e.g., stratified random samples, the variance of subgroups, strata or clusters must be taken care prior to estimation of the variability in population.
- If descriptive statistics are to be used, e.g., mean, frequencies, then nearly any sample size will suffice.
- A good sample size, e.g., 200-500, is compulsory for multiple regression, analysis of covariance, or log-linear analysis, which might be performed for more precise state impact assessment.
- The sample size should be appropriate for the analysis that is planned.
- In addition, an adjustment in the sample size may be needed to accommodate a comparative analysis of subgroups (e.g., such as an evaluation of program participants with nonparticipants). Sudman (1976) suggests that a minimum of 100 elements is needed for each major group or subgroup in the sample and for each minor subgroup, a sample of 20 to 50 elements is necessary. Similarly, Kish (1965) says that 30 to 200 elements are sufficient when the attribute is present 20 to 80 percent of the time (i.e., the distribution approaches normality). On the other hand, skewed distributions can result in serious departures from normality even for moderate size samples (Kish, 1965:17). Then a larger sample or a census is required.
- Many researchers commonly add 10% to the sample size to compensate for persons that the researcher is unable to contact.
- The sample size also is often increased by 30% to compensate for non response."[1].

5 -G.Mixner 1998

Different sampling methods (Strategies): a. Census sampling:

It is study the entire population. A **census** is the procedure of systematically acquiring and recording information about the members of a given population. It is a regularly occurring and official count of a particular population. The term is used mostly in connection with national population and housing censuses; other common censuses include agriculture, business, and traffic censuses. In the latter cases the elements of the 'population' are farms, businesses, and so forth, rather than people.[21].

*NOTICE: In most of the books the sampling method is divided only in two categories (Probability and non probability) and census in not considered as a sampling method.

b. Probability or Random sampling:

6 -G.Mixner 1998

-In probability sampling all elements have same chance to be chosen. However, in non-random sampling some elements don't have any chance for being selected.

-It is used in quantitative research.

b.1: Simple random sampling:

In this kind of sampling, table or calculator is used to generate random numbers. For example in some calculators (#) is hired for creating a random number or in Excel we can hire the related command {=rand (selected value)} for generating random numbers. Then, the sample elements are picked up. **Simple random sampling** refers to a sampling method that has the following properties.

• The population consists of *N* objects.
• The sample consists of *n* objects.
• All possible samples of *n* objects are equally likely to occur.

The main benefit of simple random sampling is that it guarantees that the sample chosen is representative of the population. This ensures that the statistical conclusions will be valid.

There are many ways to obtain a simple random sample. One way would be the lottery method. Each of the *N* population members is assigned a unique number. The numbers are placed in a bowl and thoroughly mixed. Then, a blind-folded researcher selects *n* numbers. Population members having the selected numbers are included in the sample. [11].

It is one of the most unbiased ways for choosing samples. However, it can be so expensive and time taking. Since, the amount of population and its dispersion is different from one population to others. Furthermore, sometimes we are faced with a wide population in a vast area.

b.2: Systematic sampling:

This is random sampling with a system! From the sampling frame, a starting point is chosen at random, and thereafter at regular intervals. For example, suppose you want to sample 8 houses from a street of 120 houses. 120/8=15, so every 15th house is chosen after a random starting point between 1 and 15. If the random starting point is 11, then the houses selected are 11, 26, 41, 56, 71, 86, 101, and 116. If there were 125 houses, 125/8=15.625, so should you take every 15th house or every 16th house? If you take every 16th house, 8*16=128 so there is a risk that the last house chosen does not exist. To overcome this, random starting point should be between 1 and 10. On the other hand if you take every 15th house, 8*15=120 so the last five houses will never be selected. The random starting point should now be between 1 and 20 to ensure that every house has some chance of being selected. In a random sample every member of the population has an equal chance of being chosen, which clearly not the case here is, but in practice a systematic sample is almost always acceptable as being random. [12]

Systematic sampling is more arranged and as a result it is easier than simple random sampling. However, hidden patterns in population can cause to some problems in process of sampling.

b.3: Stratified sampling:

In a stratified sample the sampling frame is divided into non-overlapping groups or strata, e.g. geographical areas, age-groups, genders. A sample is taken from each stratum, and when this sample is a simple random sample it is referred to as **stratified random sampling**.[12].

The gotten samples are more accurate. Since, similar members are put in same strata .In some studies which are involved with different industries or different age groups of people , the stratified sampling can be more convenient than other methods and it can cover greater area of population than its counterparts. However, putting the similar members in same strata must be done accurately .So , it is more complex than simple random sampling.

b.4: Cluster sampling:

In cluster sampling the units sampled are chosen in clusters, close to each other. Examples are households in the same street, or successive items off a production line. The population is divided into clusters, and some of these are then chosen at random. Within each cluster units are then chosen by simple random sampling or some other methods. Ideally the clusters chosen should be dissimilar so that the sample is as representative of the population as possible. [12].

With hiring this method amount of money and time which is spent for sampling can be reduced. However, its sampling error is high. Furthermore, the representativeness of the whole population in this method is less than simple random method.

b.5: Other sampling techniques:

Multistage sampling: In this kind of sampling we combine more than one kind of sampling together, e.g. combining the cluster sampling and simple random.

c. Non-probability sampling:

- It is used in quantitative research.

The most important advantage of these methods is related to the time and expense which is spent. These methods are more time and expense saver than random methods. However , the degree of error and accuracy of sampling method are higher and lower than random methods respectively.

c.1: Accidental, Haphazard or Convenience Sampling:

The subjects are selected just because they are easiest to recruit for the study and the researcher did not consider selecting subjects that are representative of the entire population. In all forms of research, it would be ideal to test the entire population, but in most cases, the population is just too large that it is impossible to include every individual. This is the reason why most researchers rely on sampling techniques like convenience sampling, the most common of all sampling techniques. Many researchers prefer this sampling technique because it is fast, inexpensive, easy and the subjects are readily available. One of the most common examples of convenience sampling is using student volunteers as subjects for the research. Another example is using subjects that are selected from a clinic, a class or an institution that is easily accessible to the researcher. A more concrete example is choosing five people from a class or choosing the first five names from the list of patients. In these examples, the researcher inadvertently excludes a great proportion of the population. A convenience sample is either a collection of subjects that are accessible or a self selection of individuals willing to participate which is exemplified by your volunteers. [13].

c.2: *Judgmental sampling:*

Judgmental sampling is a non-probability sampling technique where the researcher selects units to be sampled based on their knowledge and professional judgment. His type of sampling technique is also known as *purposive sampling* and *authoritative sampling*. Purposive sampling is used in cases where the specialty of an authority can select a more representative sample that can bring more accurate results than by using other probability sampling techniques. The process involves nothing but purposely handpicking individuals from the population based on the authority's or the researcher's knowledge and judgment. In a study wherein a researcher wants to know what it takes to graduate summa cum laude in college, the only people who can give the researcher first hand advise are the individuals who graduated summa cum laude. With this very specific and very limited pool of individuals that can be considered as a subject, the researcher must use judgmental sampling. [13].

c.3: *Quota sampling:*

Quota sampling is a non-probability sampling technique wherein the assembled sample has the same proportions of individuals as the entire population with respect to known characteristics, traits or focused phenomenon.

- The first step in non-probability quota sampling is to divide the population into exclusive subgroups.
- Then, the researcher must identify the proportions of these subgroups in the population; this same proportion will be applied in the sampling process.
- Finally, the researcher selects subjects from the various subgroups while taking into consideration the proportions noted in the previous step.
- The final step ensures that the sample is representative of the entire population. It also allows the researcher to study traits and characteristics that are noted for each subgroup.

In a study wherein the researcher likes to compare the academic performance of the different high school class levels, its relationship with gender and socioeconomic status, the researcher first identifies the subgroups. Usually, the subgroups are the characteristics or variables of the study. The researcher divides the entire population into class levels, intersected with gender and socioeconomic status. Then, he takes note of the proportions of these subgroups in the entire population and then samples each subgroup accordingly.

c.4: Snowball Sampling:

Snowball sampling is a non-probability sampling technique that is used by researchers to identify potential subjects in studies where subjects are hard to locate and in this method selection is based on connections in a pre existing network. Researchers use this sampling method if the sample for the study is very rare or is limited to a very small subgroup of the population. This type of sampling technique works like chain referral. After observing the initial subject, the researcher asks for assistance from the subject to help identify people with a similar trait of interest. The process of snowball sampling is much like asking your subjects to nominate another person with the same trait as your next subject. The researcher then observes the nominated subjects and continues in the same way until the obtaining sufficient number of subjects. For example, if obtaining subjects for a study that wants to observe a rare disease, the researcher may opt to use snowball sampling since it will be difficult to obtain subjects. It is also possible that the patients with the same disease have a support group; being able to observe one of the members as your initial subject will then lead you to more subjects for the study.[13].

TYPES OF SNOWBALL SAMPLING

- Linear Snowball Sampling

- Exponential Non-Discriminative Snowball Sampling

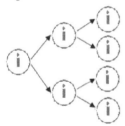

- Exponential Discriminative Snowball Sampling

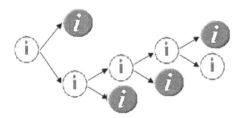

d. Theoretical sampling:

It is used in qualitative research.

- In qualitative research, new issues and things are found and explored, e.g. Regarding a new topic we have interviews with some innovators .We speak to first and second and third innovators and we can get new information .However ,with interviewing to fourth and fifth and sixth….. Persons, we can't find any other information. Thus, our sample would be 3 people.

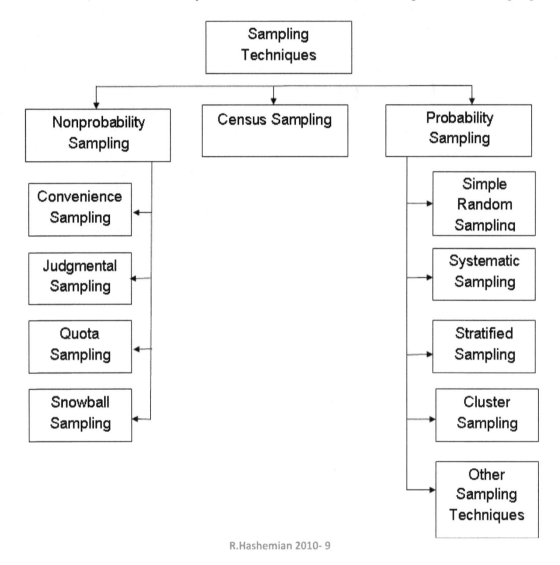

R.Hashemian 2010- 9

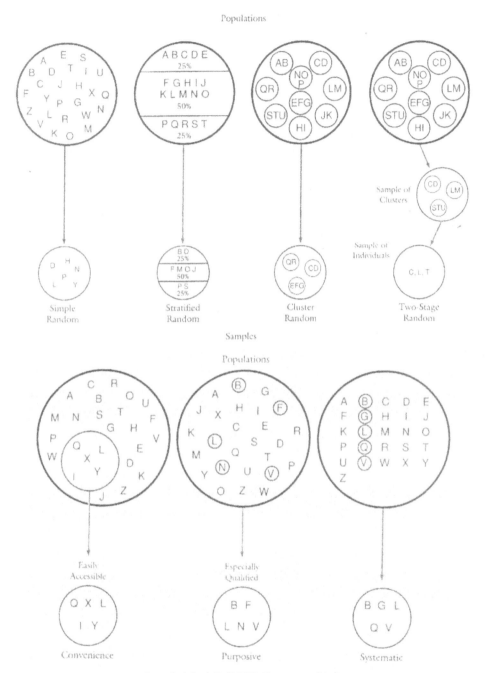

Fraenkel, Jack R. (1993).Singapore : McG

Sampling frame:

For example the list of students which sample is chosen from this list randomly. Sampling frame (synonyms: "sample frame", "survey frame") is the actual set of units from which a sample has been drawn: in the case of a simple random sample, all units from the sampling frame have an equal chance to be drawn and to occur in the sample. In the ideal case, the sampling frame should coincide with the population of interest. Consider, for instance, a survey aimed at finding the number of potential passengers for a newly arranged bus service to K.L in the population of UPM University Students. The research team has selected 500 cell phone numbers at random from a list which exists in resource center of university. Each day 100 calls are made, from Monday to Friday and during 10am to 4pm and some questions are asked.

In this example, *population* of interest is all students of the UPM University; the *sampling frame* includes only those students that satisfy all the following requirements:

⇨has a cell phone;

⇨the cell phone number exist in the resource center;

⇨likely to not to be in class from 8am to 5pm from Monday to Friday;

⇨Not a person who refuses to answer all telephone surveys.

The *sampling frame* in this case definitely differs from the *population*. For example, it under-represents the categories which either have no a cell phone (e.g. the most poor), have an unlisted number, and who were in class at the time of calls (e.g. students who don't answer their mobile phone during lecturer), who don't like to participate in telephone interviews (e.g. more busy students). Such differences between the sampling frame and the population of interest is a main cause of bias in surveys and other methods aimed at random sampling.[14].

A *sample frame* is a list that includes every member of the population from which a sample is to be taken. Without some form of *sample frame*, a random sample of a population, other than an extremely small population, is impossible. When a list of the population of interest is not available, an alternate method for capturing the population must be found. Most surveys carried out by governmental statistical agencies rely on a sample frame that is composed of maps that partition the entire country into *enumeration areas*. In that case, a multi-stage sample design is required. Enumeration areas are first randomly sampled, and then individual housing units are sampled from within the enumeration areas. Finally, individuals are sampled from within the housing units.

Even though the set of maps of enumeration areas is not a list of individuals in the population, it is still considered a sample frame. In that case, however, it is a sample frame of individuals that reside in housing units, not of the total population. Any individual who does not live in a housing unit, for example, a homeless person, is not covered by the sample frame. . Furthermore, a complete list of all the units of the population is called the sampling frame. A unit of population is a relative term. If all the workers in a factory make a population, a single worker is a unit of the population. If all the factories in a country are being studied for some purpose, a single factory is a unit of the population of factories. The sampling frame contains all the units of the population. It is to be defined clearly as to which units are to be included in the frame. The frame provides a base for the selection of the sample. [15].

Bonus points:

Some of the most common used statistical symbols are as below.

Symbol	What it Represents
X	variable
$\bar{X}$	sample mean
μ	population mean
δ	sample standard deviation
$δ^2$	sample variance
σ	population standard deviation
$σ^2$	population variance
p̂	sample proportion
p	population proportion
q	1-p
n	sample size
α	significance level
SE	standard error (σ of a sampling distribution)

Chapter 3: Probability Distributions

What is probability Distribution?

7 -G.Mixner 1998

Standard or established pattern or behavior of a characteristic (Random variable). A statistical function that describes all the possible values and likelihoods that a random variable can take within a given range. This range will be between the minimum and maximum statistically possible values, but where the possible value is likely to be plotted on the probability distribution depends on a number of factors, including the distributions mean, standard deviation, skewness and kurtosis. Academics and fund managers alike may determine a particular stock's probability distribution to determine the possible returns that the stock may yield in the future. The stock's history of returns, which can be measured on any time interval, will likely be comprised of only a fraction of the stock's returns, which will subject the analysis to sampling error. By increasing the sample size, this error can be dramatically reduced. [16].

Two broad categories of probability distribution:
a. Discrete distributions:
Characteristics under study (Random variable) assumes discrete or integer values. e.g.: Binominal distribution, Poisson distribution, Negative exponential.
b. Continuous distributions:
Characteristics under study (Random variable) assume any real value .e.g.: Normal distribution, t distribution, F distribution.

Normal distribution (Guassian distribution or bell- shaped distribution)
-It is symmetrical (Mean= Median=Mode)
-Two parameters which describe normal distribution are mean and standard deviation.
-Normal curve doesn't touch the x-axis.
-Total area under the normal curve is equal to one. (Each half is 0.5)
-Area under the normal curve denotes probability.

-X axis stands for characteristic under study and Y axis stands for relative frequency (Frequency means how many times that particular thing happened)
-Total area under normal curve equals 1.

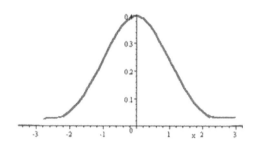

Standard Normal Curve $\mu = 0$, $\sigma = 1$

Example1-3:

Demand	Frequency	Relative Frequency
100	20	20/100=0.2
150	40	40/100=0.4
250	30	30/100=0.3
300	10	10/100=0.1
	Total=100	

The amount of demand for 20 weeks was 100 units.
The amount of demand for 40 weeks was 150 units.
The amount of demand for 30 weeks was 250 units.
The amount of demand for 10 weeks was 300 units.

Truncated normal distribution:

In probability and statistics, the **truncated normal distribution** is the probability distribution of a normally distributed random variable whose value is either bounded below or above (or both). The truncated normal distribution has wide applications in statistics and econometrics. For example, it is used to model the probabilities of the binary outcomes in the Probit model and to model censored data in the Tobit model. [17 , 27].

Example2-3:

 Among a group of people the shortest person is 4 fits height and the tallest person is 7 fits height. Thus, the normal curve will be between 4 and 7.

Example3-3:

-Area under the normal curve between $\mu + \sigma$ and $\mu - \sigma$=0.65
-Area under the normal curve between $\mu + 2\sigma$ and $\mu - 2\sigma$=0.95
-Area under the normal curve between $\mu + 3\sigma$ and $\mu - 3\sigma$=99.67
While σ stands for standard deviation.

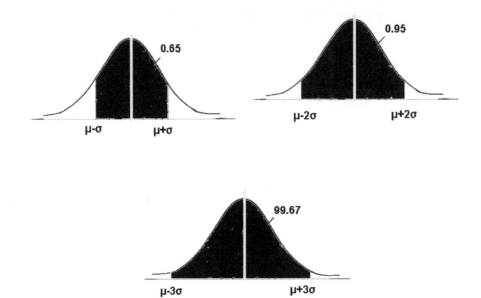

Three views which introduce the probability approach are:

1) Classical probability
2) Experimental probability:
3) Subjective probability:
- In this kind of probability, we can't do any test or calculation as well as it is in based on experimental judgment.

Sampling distribution:

Definition: Distribution of all possible samples is called sampling distribution.
- If the parameter that is studied was mean, we would have sampling distribution of means.
- In reality, sampling distribution cannot be constructed. It is a theoretical concept, but properties of sampling distribution can be practically used in statistical tests.
- Sampling distribution of means: Distribution of means of all possible samples.
- The mean of sampling distribution= $\mu_{\bar{x}}$
Standard deviation of sampling distribution =Standard error = $\sigma_{\bar{x}}$

$$\sigma_{\bar{x}} = \frac{\sigma}{\sqrt{n}} \qquad n = sample\ size\ , \sigma = standard\ deviation\ of\ population$$

Example4-3:

A=1.0	B=1.5	C=2.0	D=2.5

AB=1+1.5/2=1.25, AC=1.5, AD=1.75, BC=1.75, BD=2, CD=2.25

Sample means	Population
1.25	1
1.5	1.5
1.75	2
1.75	2.5
2	-
2.25	-
$\mu_{\bar{x}}=1.75$	$\mu = 1.75$

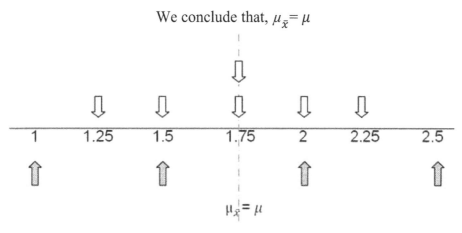

We conclude that, $\mu_{\bar{x}} = \mu$

R.Hashemian 2010- 10

As it can be seen from the illustration, dispersion in sample means is less than dispersion in population.

- With taking larger sample, standard error is decreased.

- $\sigma_{\bar{x}} = \frac{\sigma}{\sqrt{n}}$ (As n is increased, standard error is decreased as well as accuracy in estimating population parameter is increased and vice versa)

Link between population distribution and sampling distribution:

Property 1: If the distribution of population is normal with mean μ and standard deviation σ .Then, sampling distribution of means is also normal with mean $\mathbf{\mu}_{\bar{x}} = \mathbf{\mu}$ and standard error while n stands for sample size is,

$$\sigma_{\bar{x}} = \frac{\sigma}{\sqrt{n}} \, ,$$

Property2: Central limit theorem: Mean μ and standard deviation σ_i of the population distribution are arbitrary, as long as the sample size is larger than 30(n>=30).Sampling distribution is approximately normal with $\mu_{\bar{x}} = \mu$, $\sigma_{\bar{x}} = \frac{\sigma}{\sqrt{n}}$ while n stands for sample size.

Bonus Points:

For writing an abstract follow format below.
-Purpose of study
-Very brief background
-Design/Methodology/Approach
-Findings
-Theoretical and practical implications (very brief)
-Limitations of study and directions for future research (optional)
Abstract for Thesis/Dissertation ➜ 300 words
Abstract for research paper ➜ 150 words

Chapter 4: Inferential Statistics

Estimator: Sample statistic which is used to estimate the population parameter.
Estimate: The numerical value.
Estimation error: If the sample was not representative of the population, underestimating and overestimating happens in estimation process. Thus, the estimation error can be happened.

Different Types of Estimation:

a. Point estimation:
- Single numerical value
- Suffers from sampling error
- There are chances that parameter values maybe over or underestimated.
- For decreasing estimation error, interval estimation is used in behalf of point estimation as well as lower and upper limit is determined.

b. Interval estimation:

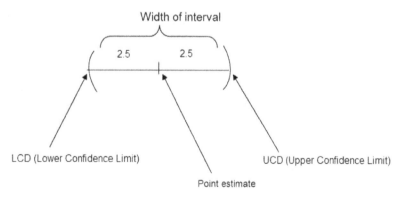

R.Hashemian 2010- 11

Two parameters which are required to construct interval estimates:
1) Confidence level:
2) Standard error:

Example1-4:

If it was asked that how much is the average of students CGPA in a classroom, with hundred percent confidence it can be said which it is a number between 0 and 100. However, if the width of the interval was reduced, the degree of assurance would be decreased. Thus, confidence level plays important role in interval estimation.

- Degree of confidence that a researcher wants to have in constructing the interval is called confidence level and it denotes the probability that actual population parameter values lies within the interval.
- In SPSS the default number for confidence level is equal to 95%.
- Width of interval is increased with increasing in confident level.
- Width of interval is increased with increasing in standard error.

Example2-4:

The GSS asks respondents to rate their political views on a seven point scale, where 1=extremely liberal, 4 = moderate, and 7=extremely conservative. A researcher analyzing data from the 2004 GSS gets software output. [18]

Variable	N	Mean	St.Dev	SE Mean	99% CI
Polviews	1294	4.33	1.39	0.0387	(4.13,4.33)

$$\frac{1.39}{\sqrt{12.94}} = 0.0387$$

$$4.13 \left(\begin{matrix} 4.23 \\ \bullet \end{matrix} \right) 4.33$$

We are 99%confident that the actual mean value of variable, Polview will lie between 4.13 and 4.33.

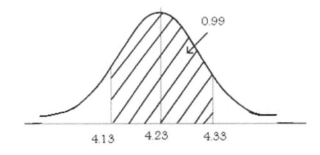

R.Hashemian 2010- 12

*NOTICE: If sample size was >20000, the population is considered infinitive. However, sample size like 350, is suitable for large population.

$$* \Rightarrow UCL = \bar{X} + (Z_{C.L} * \sigma_{\bar{X}})$$
$$* \Rightarrow LCL = \bar{X} + (Z_{C.L} * \sigma_{\bar{X}})$$

Good estimators:

Uniformly Minimum Variance Unbiased Estimator (UMVUE)

- Sample mean is a good estimator for population mean.
- Sample standard deviation is a good estimator for population standard deviation.
- Sample proportion is a good estimator for population proportion.

*NOTICE :(Refer to chapter one)

$$A. \sigma^2 = \frac{\sum(x-\mu)^2}{n} \qquad\qquad B. \sigma^2 = \frac{\sum(x-\bar{x})^2}{n-1}$$

With equation B, we can get more precise answer than equation A.

Chapter 5: Testing of Hypothesis

What is Hypothesis?

Hypothesis is a statement about a population parameter .In testing of hypothesis ,we make a statement about the parameter and by taking a sample and testing ,we verify if the statement which we have made about the population parameter is correct or not. Hypothesis must be precise and concise as well as testable. It is a statement about a population parameter. A sample is taken and tested if the statement which was made can be supported or not.

For instance, a medicine producing company has a claim which 95% of sick people that consume its products, are treated. This is a hypothesis and must be tested.

Two statements (hypothesis) are made. Each statement is opposite of the other one. While testing hypothesis, only one statement or hypothesis will be supported. Other statement will not be supported .e.g.

- New training program effectiveness is better than the effectiveness of old training program.

- New training program effectiveness is not better than the effectiveness of old training program.

One of them is called Null hypothesis (H0) and another one is called Alternate hypothesis (H1or Ha).

*NOTICE:

*H1or Ha is any claim that should be tested.

*Null hypothesis and alternative hypothesis must be opposite.

Nullifying means to make void, so when the hypothesis we are testing is not supported, we are nullifying the claim and that's why we call it null hypothesis.

*NOTICE: Nullify means make null or invalidation.

Testing of hypothesis starts with the assumption that H0 is true. If there is overwhelming evidence to indicate that alternate hypothesis is supported, then H0 is rejected. If there is no overwhelming evidence to indicate that alternate hypothesis is supported, then H0 is not rejected.

Some examples for alternative hypothesis:

H1: There is a positive relationship between job satisfaction and job performance.

H1: There is a negative relationship between emotional exhibition and job satisfaction.

H1: Job satisfaction mediates the relationship between personal accomplishment and job performance.

H1: Environment moderates the relationship between strategic alliance motives and interdependence between alliance partners.

H1: The average efficiency level of female is more than the average efficiency level of male.

*NOTICE: Strategic alliance is league created for mutual strategic benefit.

The steps involved in testing of hypothesis:

1) Based on the research problem, state H0 and H1. (By researcher)

2) Based on the significant level define the rejection region. (-Rejection region is the region that specifies the values that leads to rejection of H0) (-Researcher specifies significant level)

3) Based on the sample information, compute statistic test. (Done by SPSS)

4) Check if test statistic falls in the rejection region or not. (By researcher)

5) Conclude whether to support H1 or not support H1. (-Write conclusion) (-By researcher)

Different Types of Errors in Testing Hypothesis:

In a trial, we have the following hypothesis, (H).

H0: the person is innocent (not guilty).

H1: the person is guilty.

True state of nature (Refer to Illustration Below):

	Innocent	Guilty
Innocent	Correct decision	Wrong decision **Type 2 error**
Guilty	Wrong decision **Type 1 error**	Correct decision

R.Hashemian 2010- 13

Type I error: Reject H0 when H0 is true

Type II error: Do not reject H0 when H1 is true

Probability of committing type I error is showed by α.

Probability of committing type II error is showed by β.

Generally, type I error is controlled. Typical values probability of committing type I error (α) is equal to 0.05.

α: maximum level of type I error allowed in the experiment and its default value is equal to 0.05(5%).

Two aspects that help to take decision in testing of a hypothesis:
-Rejection region (specified by α)
-Test statistic (obtained from sample)

What is P-Value?

P-value stands for **probability value** and it has to be a number between zero and one.
There are different definitions regarding this term.
For example in **Fundamentals of Biostatistics, Volume 1 By Bernard A. Rosner**, it is described as follows. [23]
"The p-value for any hypothesis test is α level at which we would be indifferent between accepting or rejecting H0 given the sample data at hand. That is, the p-value is the α level at which the given value of the test statistic (such as t) is on the borderline between the acceptance and rejection regions. (p.232)
The p-value can also be thought of as the probability of obtaining a test statistic as extreme as or more extreme than the actual test statistic obtained , given that the null hypothesis is true" .(p.233)
Or **Hogg, R.V, Tanis, E.A"Probability and Statistical Inference", 5th edition, p-352** describes it as follows, [24]
"The p-value associated with a test is the probability that we obtained the observed value of the test statistics or value that is more extreme in the direction of the alternative hypothesis calculated when the null hypothesis is true."
Remember the example which a person was put in trial for murdering someone. Imagine the person was not guilty(was innocent). However, juries rejected the null hypothesis (The person was innocent) in favor of alternative hypothesis (he was guilty) and put the person in jail. So, they made a mistake. We call it type one error. The p-value assesses the information which we have and according to that information we decide to reject or fail to reject the null hypothesis.
The significance level is the amount of chance in a test which someone has to make mistake. If the gotten p-value was less than the significance level, the null hypothesis is rejected. However we want the amount of this probability (Making mistake) to be low. Usually, the amount of significance level is considered 0.05(5%) and maybe its clue is on a statement from an article belong to **Fisher (1926)** which says, [25]
"If one in twenty does not seem high enough odds, we may, if we prefer it, draw the line at one in fifty (the 2 per cent point), or one in a hundred (the 1 per cent point). Personally, the writer prefers to set a low standard of significance at the 5 per cent point, and ignore entirely all results which fail to reach this level. A scientific fact should be regarded as experimentally established only if a properly designed experiment rarely fails to give this level of significance." (p. 504)
So, we will reject the null hypothesis if the p-value is less than 5 % and our significance level is 5% too. You could use your own significance level. It doesn't have to be 5 %.You could use 1

% or any other value. It depends on the significance level which you would like to use. But as the rule of thumb, if the p-value is low the null hypothesis must go or reject the null hypothesis if the p value is low.

Remember what we are doing in statistical hypothesis test is collecting evidence to see whether the null hypothesis can be rejected or not. So we don't want to prove the accuracy of null hypothesis.

Notice that the fail the reject of the null hypothesis will be so easy if the sample size is very small and variation is huge.

The steps involved in p-value method are as below.

1. Choose a statistical test.

2. Calculate the test statistic on the basis of the probability distribution function.

3. Obtain the p- value from the test statistic probability table or a computer software.

4. Compare the p-value with the significance level to determine whether the null hypothesis should be rejected.

*NOTICE: Significance level specifications are,
- The significance level of a test is the probability of α error.
- The level of α error which one is willing to tolerate.
- Usually set at 0.05, but can be other arbitrary values as well.

Chapter 6: Two tailed test vs. One tailed test

Two-sided (Two -tailed) Test

In this test the values of the parameter which is studied by the alternative hypothesis are allowed to be either greater than or less than the values of the parameter under the null hypothesis.

Example: Hospital A was the only cardiovascular center in city X .The management of this center has claim that each year 85% of their patients which leave the hospital can go back to their normal life. Newly another cardiovascular center which is called B is opened in the same city. And it was found that from the 200 patients which was selected as a sample from B for duration of one year, around 88 % could go back to their normal life after leaving the hospital while standard deviation is 4%.Is there any difference between the rate of the people who went back to their normal life in hospital B in compare with the rest of the patients which went back to their normal life in hospital A?

The question here is,

Is there any **difference** between the rate of the people who went back to their normal life in hospital B in compare with the rest of the patients which went back to their normal life in hospital A?

This is a two tailed test .Since; we are going to test if the mean is either **above** or **below** the 85%.So, if α was 0.05,the distribution would be like this.

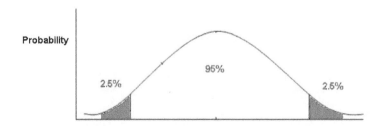

One-sided (One -tailed) Test
In this test the values of the parameter which is studied by the alternative hypothesis are allowed to be either greater than or less than the values of the parameter under the null hypothesis, **but not both**.

In previous example if the question was, Is the rate of patients who went back to the normal life **greater than** 85%?
This is one tailed test. Since, we are testing only to see whether the mean is **greater than** 85%.

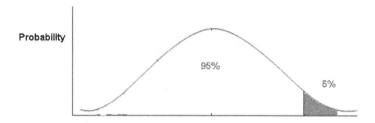

In previous example if the question was,Is the rate of patients who went back to the normal life **less than** 85%?This is one tailed test. Since, we are testing only to see whether the mean is **less than** 85%.

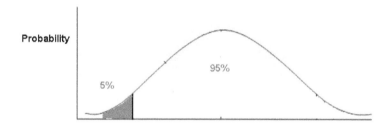

An overview to Testing of Means and Relationships:

```
                        ┌─────────────────┐
                        │ Testing of Means │
                        └─────────────────┘
              ┌───────────────┼───────────────┐
              ↓               ↓               ↓
     ┌──────────────┐  ┌──────────┐  ┌──────────────┐
     │ One Sample   │  │ Two      │  │ More Than    │
     │ T Test       │  │ Samples  │  │ Two          │
     └──────────────┘  └──────────┘  │ Samples      │
                         │      │     └──────────────┘
              ┌──────────┘      │            │
              ↓                 ↓            ↓
     ┌──────────────┐  ┌──────────────┐  ┌──────────────────┐
     │ Independent  │  │ Paired       │  │ Anova(Analysis of │
     │ T Test       │  │ Sample T     │  │ Variance          │
     └──────────────┘  │ Test         │  └──────────────────┘
                       └──────────────┘
                              │
                              ↓
                  ┌──────────────────────────┐
                  │ For example, weighting    │
                  │ people before training and│
                  │ after training program    │
                  └──────────────────────────┘
```

R.Hashemian 2010- 14

*NOTICE:

If we had only one sample, but our observations were in two situations, paired sample t test is used.

For example: our sample is a group of people which use the aerobic machine for reducing their weights.

Here we have two observations.

Observation 1: the weight of person before using the machine.

Observation 2: the weight of people after using the machine.

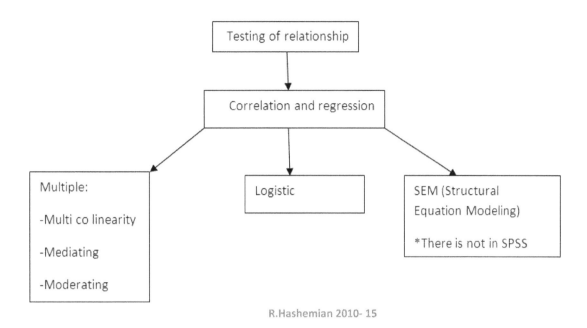

R.Hashemian 2010- 15

With doing Multiple Regression the following information can be got:
  ➢ How each individual IV is related to the DV.
  ➢ The total amount of variance explained in a dependent variable.
  ➢ Multiple regression is very dependent variable centric.
  ➢ We know nothing about how the IV's are related.

Another way to do Multiple Regression is path analysis. It is a special case of multiple regression where all the relationships among variables can be estimated simultaneously. For example the model below cannot be tested in SPSS and path analysis must be used.

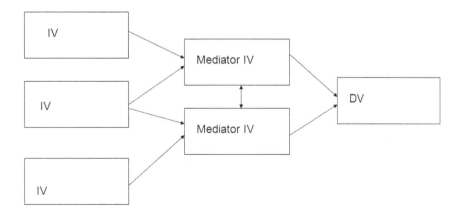

With running path analysis the followings are tested.

- Estimation of correlations among independent variables.
- Estimate regression relationships in the model
- You can make all the variables related to one another and find out what the relationship is exactly!
- All the regression analyses we did in SPSS can be done in path analysis

  Any SEM program can do path analysis.SEM programs include the followings.
- ❖ AMOS
- ❖ LISREL
- ❖ EQS

Chapter 7: An Introduction to SPSS 17

What is SPSS?

SPSS Statistics 17.0 is a exhaustive program for analyzing data. SPSS Statistics can take data from different types of files and hire them to generate tabulated reports, charts and plots of distributions and trends, descriptive statistics, and complex statistical analyses.

Executing the program:

Different ways exist for running the SPSS program. Such as, click on the related icon from desktop or running the program from program in start menu. Besides, if there was any file of SPSS in your hard disk, with clicking on it the mentioned program is activated.

5 Figure

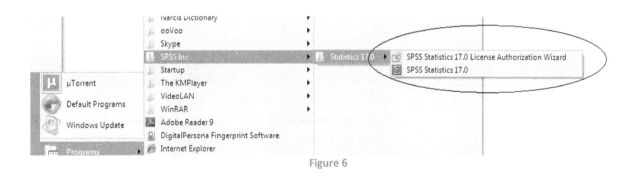

Figure 6

Entering the data in SPSS:

With clicking on SPSS icon two windows are opened. SPSS Statistics 17 and SPSS Statistics Data Editor.

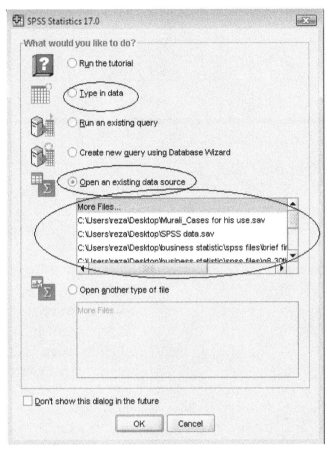

In first window, different choices are observed. The duty of each is written beside it. (Figure7).

For example, with selecting **Type in Data** and clicking on ok, the window of SPSS Statistics Data Editor is activated and the data can be entered. With choosing the Open an Existing Data Source, SPSS files which were created before are shown and you can choose any of them if it still is available.

7 Figure

There are two buttons in down part of SPSS Statistics Data Editor. They are **Variable View** and **Data View**.

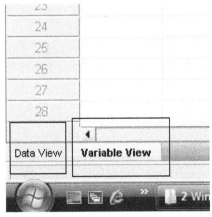

Figure8

First, the Variable View should be chosen. (Figure 8).This is because Variables are described in this part. Different parts exist in Variable View mode.

Such as **Name, Type, Width, Decimals, Label, Values, Missing, Columns, Align, Measure**.

For example, the names of variables are entered in **Name** column and if the mentioned variable came with any values, it could be described from **values** part. Such as, gender. So, for gender two values should be described including Female and Male.(Figures 9 & 10).

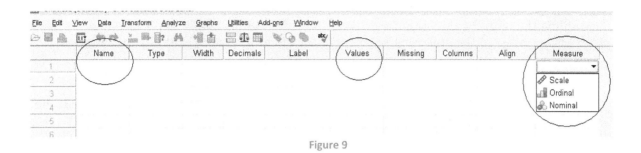

Figure 9

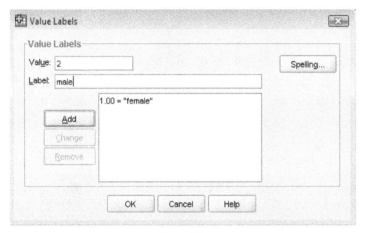

Figure10

Another important part is column of **measure**. Three choices are exist in this part. Scale, Ordinal and Nominal. According to the nature of the test as well as variable each of them can be selected.

Type: With using this part the type of investigated variable is shown. The most common used choices of this part are **Numeric** (Such as Weight, size) and **String** (Such as, Blood Group). (Figure9).

Width: The number of characters which you are allowed to enter for a variable is determined from this part. If it is a numerical value with decimals, this total width has to include a spot for each decimal, as well as one for the decimal point. For changing the width you can click in the width cell for a specific variable or the arrow keys can be used.

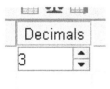

Decimals: From this part the number of decimal places which is displayed by SPSS can be adjusted. If you enter more decimals than what you described in decimal part (or computed by SPSS), the rest will be retained internally. However, it will not be displayed.

For numbers without decimal (whole numbers), you could reduce the number of decimals to zero. The number of decimals can be changed by click on decimal cell for the specific variable and type a new number or the arrow keys can be hired.

Label: The label of a variable is a text to indicate the more detailed information regarding the entered variable. Unlike the name, the label is limited to 255 characters and may contain spaces and punctuation. For instance, if there is a variable for each question on a questionnaire, you would type the question as the variable label. Changing the variable can be done with clicking within the related cell.

Missing: We sometimes want to signal to SPSS that data should be treated as missing, even though there is some other numerical code recorded instead of the data actually being missing (in which case SPSS displays a single period -- this is also called SYSTEM MISSING data).

In this example, after clicking on the ... button in the Missing cell, we declared "9", "99", and "999" all to be treated by SPSS as missing (i.e. these values will be ignored)

Figure11

Columns: The columns property tells SPSS how wide the column should be for each variable. Don't confuse this one with width, which indicates how many digits of the number will be displayed. The column size indicates how much space is allocated rather than the degree to which it is filled.(Figure 9)

Align: The alignment property indicates whether the information in the Data View should be left-justified, right-justified, or centered.

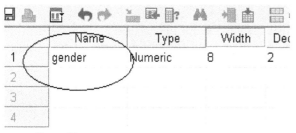

Figure12

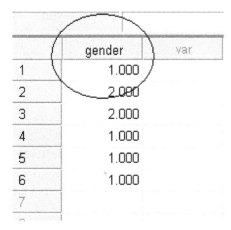

In the data view mode, the name of variables which were described in Variable View mode , will be observable. (Figure 12&13).

And we can enter the related data to that variable in column belong to it. (Figure13).

13 Figure

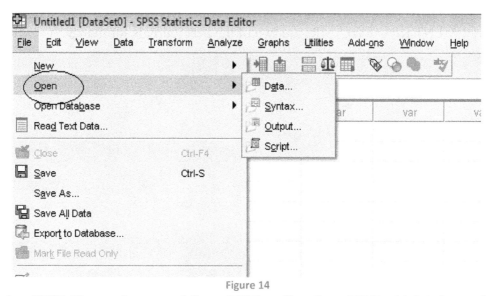

Figure 14

The existing SPSS file can be opened from SPSS toolbar from FILE which is located in top of the window as well as the new file can be created with click on NEW in toolbar in FILE part. (Figure 14)

Different errors in SPSS:

The name of each SPSS variable in a given file must be unique; it must start with a letter; it may have up to 8 characters (including letters, numbers, and the underscore _ (note that certain key words are reversed and may not be used as variable names, e.g., "compute", "sum", and so forth). To change an existing name, click in the cell containing the name, highlight the part you want to change, and type in the replacement. To create a new variable name, click in the first empty row under the name column and type a new (unique) variable name.

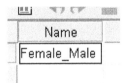

Notice that we can enter "Female_Male" but not "Female-Male" and not "Female Male". The hyphen gets interpreted as subtraction (Female minus Male) by SPSS, and the space confuses SPSS as to how many variables are being named. [22].

Bonus points:

Notice that all articles from all journals are not reliable. Thus, try to study only articles which are sourced by authentic as well as highly ranked journals. For checking the ranking of journals, you can refer to some websites such as ABDC JOURNAL LIST, ERA JOURNAL RANKING. For example, follow the link below.

http://www.abdc.edu.au/3.43.0.0.1.0.htm

INTERNATIONAL JOURNAL OF MANAGEMENT REVIEWS (IJMR) and ACADEMY OF MANAGEMENT REVIEW(AMR) are two of the best journals for management fields.

Chapter 8: One Sample T Test

What is One Sample T Test?

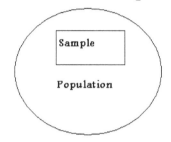

R.Hashemian 2010- 16

*NOTICE:

$\mu \rightarrow$ mean	
$\sigma^2 \rightarrow$ variance	
$\sigma \rightarrow$ standard deviation	
Sample mean $\rightarrow \bar{X}, \bar{Y}$	Sample Statistics
Sample variance $\rightarrow \delta^2$	
Sample standard deviation $\rightarrow \delta$	

For testing the hypothesis in single sample test, the following process is hired.

H0: $\mu \leq \mu$ H0   H0: $\mu \geq \mu$ H0   H0: $\mu = \mu$ H0
H1: $\mu > \mu$ H0   OR   H0: $\mu < \mu$ H0   OR   H0: $\mu \neq \mu$ H0

Example1-8:

If a new process for mining copper is to be put into full-time operation, it must produce an average of more than 50 tons of ore per day.A15-day trial period gave the results shown in the accompanying table.

	1	2	3	4	5
Day Yield(tons)	57.8	58.3	50.3	38.5	47.9
	6	7	8	9	10
Day Yield(tons)	157.0	38.6	140.2	39.3	138.7
	11	12	13	14	15
Day Yield(tons)	49.2	139.7	48.3	59.2	49.7

a. Estimated the typical amount of ore produced by the mine using both a point estimate and a 95% confidence interval.

b. Is there significant evidence that on a typical day the mine produces more than 50 tons of ore? Test by using α=.05.

Let μ denote the average yield of ore per day.

H0: $\mu \leq 50$

H1: $\mu > 50$

First, we click on variable view mode button and write the word yield in name column. Each column refers to variable and each row refers to responders.

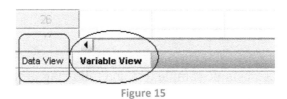

Figure 15

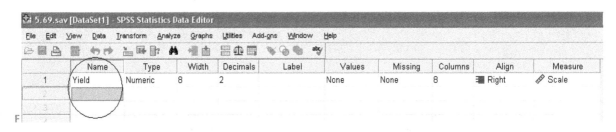

Figure 16

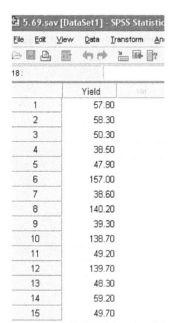

Then, we click on data view button and enter the related data. (Figures 15 & 17)

Figure 17

Next, from the analyze menu and from compare means, we choose the one sample t test.

18 Figure

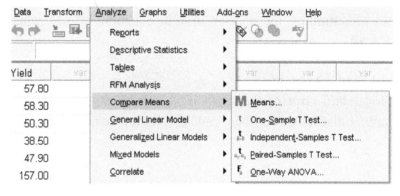

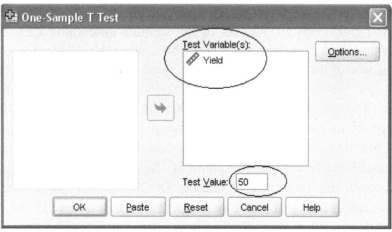

Figure 19

Then, we move the yield to test variable in right column. The test value should be adjusted to 50. Since, in question and in part b is written more than 50 tons.

Finally, we click on ok button and get the output.

One-Sample Statistics

	N	Mean	Std. Deviation	Std. Error Mean
Yield	15	74.1800	44.18138	11.40758

The first table from the top denotes the descriptive statistics.

$$\text{Standard error} = \sigma_{\bar{X}} = \frac{\sigma}{\sqrt{n}} = \frac{44.18138}{\sqrt{15}} = 11.40, \ n = \text{sample size,}$$

Before continuing the answer of this question let see what is the **STANDARD ERROR MEAN?**

Standard Error Mean:

The standard error of the mean is shown by $\sigma_{\bar{X}}$. It stands for the standard deviation of the sampling distribution of the mean. The formula can be expressed as follows:

$$\sigma_{\bar{X}} = \frac{\sigma}{\sqrt{n}}$$

where σ is the standard deviation of the original distribution and n is the sample size (the number of scores each mean is based upon). This formula does not assume a normal distribution. However, many of the uses of the formula do assume a normal distribution. The formula shows that the larger the sample size, the smaller the standard error of the mean. More specifically, the size of the standard error of the mean has reversely relationship with the square root of sample size. For better understanding the issue let introduce it with an example,

In pic A below (it is our original distribution) we can see a crazy distribution. Let take samples from this distribution. For example take 10 samples (n=10) and average them. Do this for several times (take 10 samples from this distribution several times and average them). Then, Plot all these averages and we can get the graph B. Again take samples from the distribution in picture A .However, this time take 20 samples (n=20) and do this several times and plot the averages .So we can get the graph C. Plot in graph C is tighter than B and distribution in graph C more normal than graph B. Let take larger sample size. For example n=100.The plot comes as picture D. The distribution for picture D is more normal than others and its standard deviation is so low.

So as you increase your number of samples your distribution comes more normal as well as the standard deviation is reduced.

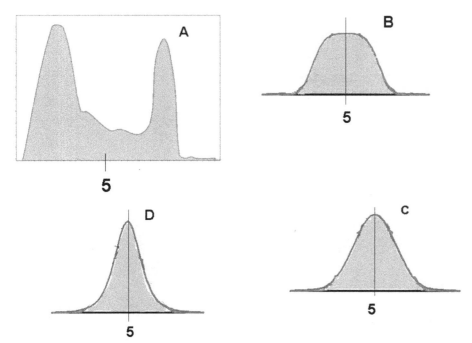

Notice that mean of the distribution in picture A is considered to be 5 and let say all distributions above have same mean. The mean for A (true mean) is shown with μ and the mean for B, C and D (mean of our mean or mean of our sample mean) are shown with $\mu_{\bar{X}}$.

Let say we know the standard deviation of our Original probability density function (original distribution) which is shown by σ and suppose we don't know the standard deviation of the distributions B , C and D .(Notice that the standard deviation is square root of Variance).

So, we can get the standard deviation as well as variance of B or C or D as follows.

$$\sigma_{\bar{X}}^{2} = \frac{\sigma^{2}}{n}$$

Standard deviation of the sampling distribution of the sample mean which is often called **Standard deviation of the mean** and it is also called **standard error of the mean** is calculated as follows.

$$\sigma_{\bar{X}} = \frac{\sigma}{\sqrt{n}}$$

Answer for example 1-8 Continues,

We cannot say which mean (74.18) is significant for n=15.Since, standard error is big. Thus, we go to second table.

One-Sample Test

				Test Value = 50			
	t	df	Sig. (2-tailed)	Mean Difference	95% Confidence Interval of the Difference		
						Lower	Upper
Yield	2.120	14	.052	24.18000		-.2868	48.6468

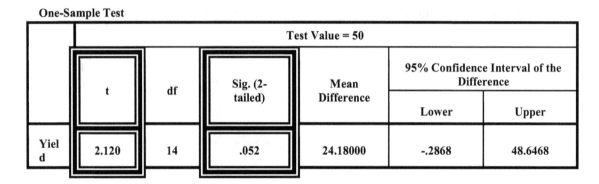

For testing hypothesis, the most important value is p-value or sig. (2-tailed).

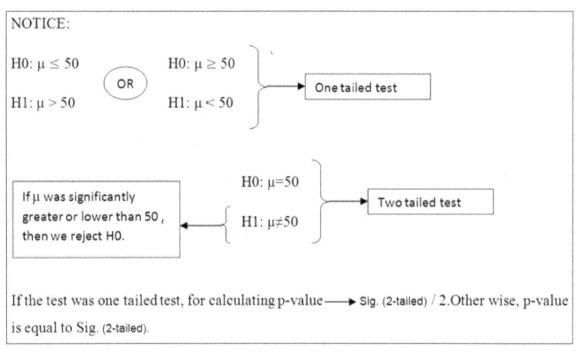

NOTICE:

H0: $\mu \leq 50$ H0: $\mu \geq 50$

OR

H1: $\mu > 50$ H1: $\mu < 50$ One tailed test

If μ was significantly greater or lower than 50, then we reject H0.

H0: $\mu = 50$

H1: $\mu \neq 50$ Two tailed test

If the test was one tailed test, for calculating p-value ⟶ Sig. (2-tailed) / 2. Other wise, p-value is equal to Sig. (2-tailed).

Since, our question is one tailed. So, P-value = $\dfrac{0.052}{2} = 0.026$

Next, we will compare p-value against α:

If p-value < α → reject H0   ,   If p-value ≥ α → do not reject H0

Since p-value < ∝ then we reject H0.

Before continuing the answer of this question let see what the **DEGREE OF FREEDOM** is.

Degree of Freedom:

One of the elements in table above is df which stands for degree of freedom. We are going to introduce the meaning of df with an example.

The easiest way to understand the concept is thinking about the calculation of an average or a mean. Presume that you have 4 scores with a mean of 50.It means that $\sum X=200$.

Let choose the first score. For example 70($\sum X=70$).Second score can be whatever you want and we are totally free to choose it. Let choose 20($\sum X=70+20=90$).And we still are free to choose any number as three score. For example 45($\sum X=70+20+45=135$).However, in this point the freedom stops and we can't make any other choice except 65($\sum X=70+20+45+65=200$).This is because the sum has to come up to 200. So, when we do the average of 4 scores we have the three degree of freedom or when we average the 10 scores we have 9 degree of freedom. In general when you compute an average, you have n-1 degree of freedom. This same logic carries over when we do something like related t test which we calculate the average of differences after and before the conditions. So, if we had N items, it means the degree of freedom would be N-1 when we calculate the t statistics for related samples.

Answer for example 1-8 Continues,

The steps which has been done in this question is reviewed,

Step 1: Define the hypothesis:

H0μ≤50

H1:μ>50

Step 2: This is a one –tailed test (upper-tailed, this is because it is asked **Is there significant evidence that on a typical day the mine produces more than 50 tons of ore?**) , ∝=0.05

Step 3: Test Statistic, p-value $=\dfrac{0.052}{2}=0.026$

step4: since p-value (0.26) $<$ ∝ (0.05), we reject H0

Step 5: we have enough evidence to conclude that the average yield per day of ore is significantly greater than 50 tons/day.

Report:

In order to assess if the average yield of ore is more than 50 tons/day, we performed one-sample t test .Based on the results (t=2-120 , p-value=0.026)

We conclude that the average yield is significantly greater than 50 tons/day.

Each of mentioned values can be got manually as well .For example:

T-value$=\dfrac{74.18-50}{11.40758}=2.120$, sample mean $= 74.18$, standard error $= 11.40758$

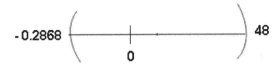

-0.2868   0   48

*NOTICE: According to the second table, df (degree of freedom) for this example is 14 or (n-1).

Z Statistic vs. T Statistic:

It is a widely discussed topic by statisticians. However, we are mentioning only some of important points as follows.

Z-statistic:

In a lot of what we are doing in inferential statistics we are trying to figure out what is the probability of getting a certain sample mean. Especially when we have a large sample size. Let draw a sampling distribution.

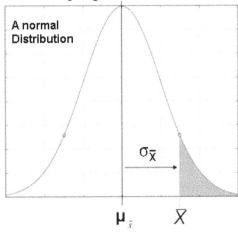

A normal Distribution

$\sigma_{\bar{x}}$

$\mu_{\bar{x}}$ $\bar{X}$

Where $\mu_{\bar{x}}$ =Mean, $\bar{x}$ =Sample mean, $\sigma_{\bar{x}}$ =Standard deviation of sampling distribution, σ=Standard deviation of population, n =Sample size

{Equation 1} Z-statistic$=\dfrac{\bar{x}-\mu_{\bar{x}}}{\sigma_{\bar{x}}}$

$\sigma_{\bar{x}}$ Stands for standard deviation of sampling distribution and it shows how many standard deviations exist above the mean.

Usually the amount of $\sigma_{\bar{x}}$ is unknown. According the central limit theorem and if the sample size was sufficient, ➜ {Equation 2} $\sigma_{\bar{x}} = \dfrac{\sigma}{\sqrt{n}}$ .We can rewrite the equation 1 and it comes

like, $\dfrac{\bar{x}-\mu_{\bar{x}}}{\frac{\sigma}{\sqrt{n}}}$ {equation 3}.This equation essentially gives the best sense for showing the amount of standard deviation from actual mean.

{Equation 4} $\text{z-statistic}=\frac{\bar{x}-\mu_{\bar{x}}}{\frac{\sigma}{\sqrt{n}}}$ ➔ with this equation and the Z table we can find how

many is the probability of getting Z or greater (extreme of results).

Sometimes we don't know how much is the value of σ .In this situation the equation comes

like (based on approximation), {Equation 5} $\text{z-statistic}\approx\frac{\bar{x}-\mu_{\bar{x}}}{\frac{s}{\sqrt{n}}}$. Where S stands for

standard deviation of sample. However, σ in equation 4 can be replaced with S ,only when n>30.Or in the other word the Z will be normally distributed.

If the sample size was less than 30, all the stated expressions and normality would not be true further.

*NOTICE: Remember that central limit theorem says,

Let X1, … Xn be a random sample from a population with mean μ and variance $\sigma2$. Then, for a large n, the mean of X $\sim N(\mu, \sigma2/n)$ even if the underlying distribution of individual observations in the population is not normal.[26].

T-distribution:

So in the case of sample less than 30 the equation comes like,

{equation6} $\text{t-distribution}\approx\frac{\bar{x}-\mu_{\bar{x}}}{\frac{s}{\sqrt{n}}}$

The rule of thumb is, if the number of your sample is more than 30 follow the equation 5.This is because in this case the sample standard deviation (δ or S) could be a good estimator of population standard deviation and the Z table can be used. However , if the number of sample was less than 30 the t distribution and t table must be used.

Example2-8:

For each girl weight was measured before and after a fixed period of treatment .the variable of interest was the change in weight that is weight at the end of study minus weight at the beginning of study. The change of weight was positive if the girl gained weight and negative if she lost weight. The treatments were designed to aid weight gain. The weight changes for 29 girls undergoing the cognitive behavioral treatment were as follows.

1.70	0.70	-0.10	-0.70	-3.50	14.90	3.50	17.10
-7.60	1.60	11.70	6.10	1.10	-4.00	20.90	-9.10
2.10	1.40	-0.30	-3.70	-1.40	-0.80	2.40	12.60
1.90	3.90	0.10	15.40	-0.7			

	ChangingWeight
1	1.70
2	0.70
3	-0.10
26	3.90
27	0.10
28	15.40
29	-0.70

Figure20

After entering the data, same procedure with previous example is hired.

The output is got as follows.

One-Sample Statistics

	N	Mean	Std. Deviation	Std. Error Mean
ChangeinWeight	29	3.0069	7.30850	1.35716

One-Sample Test

	Test Value = 0					
					95% Confidence Interval of the Difference	
	t	df	Sig. (2-tailed)	Mean Difference	Lower	Upper
ChangeinWeight	2.216	28	.035	3.00690	.2269	5.7869

Let μ denote the change in weight (after treatment-before treatment)

Step1: $H0: \mu \leq 0$
             $H1: \mu > 0$

Step 2:
  One-tailed test (upper tailed), α=0.05

Step 3:

$$\text{Test statistic, p-value} = \frac{0.035}{2} = 0.0175$$

Step 4: since p-value < α, we reject H0

Step 5: we have enough evidence to conclude that there is weight gain because of the treatment.
LCL=0.2269
UCL=5.7869
The number zero is out of the distance between LCL and UCL. Thus, H0 is rejected.

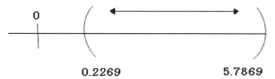

Rejecting H0→supporting H1 , Do not reject H0→not supporting H1
Based on the results of one sample t-test, we support H1 and conclude that treatment results in weight gain.

*NOTICE:
In this question if the weight of person before and after surgery had been asked, we had to use the two sample t tests.

Chapter 9: Two Sample T Tests

What are Two Sample T Tests?

8 -G.Mixner 1998

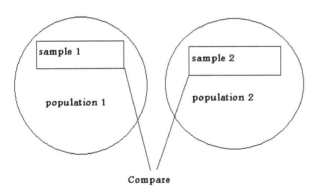

Compare

17 -R.Hashemian 2010

These tests are hired when there are two different groups with two different characteristics. We take sample from each population and compare their characteristics.(Characteristics is mean). For example, Comparing between men and women or the job satisfaction between managers and non managers.

Different types of two sample t test:
a. Independent sample t test
b. Paired sample t test

Independent sample t test:
Let μ1 denote the mean of population 1
Let μ2 denote the mean of population 2

$$H0: \mu1 \leq \mu2 \rightarrow \mu1\text{-}\mu2 \leq 0 \qquad\qquad H0: \mu1 \geq \mu2 \rightarrow \mu1\text{-}\mu2 \geq 0$$

$$H1: \mu1 > \mu2 \rightarrow \mu1\text{-}\mu2 > 0 \qquad\qquad H1: \mu1 < \mu2 \rightarrow \mu1\text{-}\mu2 < 0$$

OR

$$H0: \mu1 = \mu2 \rightarrow \mu1\text{-}\mu2 = 0$$

$$H1: \mu1 \neq \mu2 \rightarrow \mu1\text{-}\mu2 \neq 0$$

Test is done in two stages respectively:
1) Test equality of variance of two populations (levenes test)
2) Test for means
Let σ_1^2 denote variance of population 1.
Let σ_2^2 denote variance of population 2.

$$H0: \sigma_1^2 = \sigma_2^2 \Longrightarrow \begin{matrix} H0: \mu1 \geq \mu2 \\ H1: \mu1 < \mu2 \end{matrix} \; OR \; \begin{matrix} H0: \mu1 \leq \mu2 \\ H1: \mu1 > \mu2 \end{matrix} \; OR \; \begin{matrix} H0: \mu1 = \mu2 \\ H1: \mu1 \neq \mu2 \end{matrix}$$
$$H1: \sigma_1^2 \neq \sigma_2^2$$

Example1-9:

	Salary	Gender
Men	13	1
	14	1
	40	1
	10	1
Women	9	2
	45	2
	6	2
	35	2

As it is seen, there are two groups (genders) with different salaries.

Example 2-9:
A pollution-control inspector suspected that a riverside community was releasing semi treated sewage into a river and this, as a consequence, was changing the level of dissolved oxygen of

the river. To check this, he drew 15 randomly selected specimens of river water at a location above the town and another 15 specimens below. The dissolved oxygen readings, in parts per million, are given in the accompanying table.

Above Town	5.2	4.8	5.1	5.0	4.9	4.8	5.0	4.7
4.7	5.0	4.7	5.1	5.0	4.9	4.9		
Below Town	4.2	4.4	4.7	4.9	4.6	4.8	4.9	4.6
5.1	4.3	5.5	4.7	4.9	4.8	4.7		

Use the computer output shown here to answer the following questions.

Two-sample T-Test and Confidence Interval

Two-sample T for Above Town vs Below Town

	N	Mean	St Dev	SE Mean
Above To	15	4.92	0.157	0.042
Below To	15	4.74	0.320	0.084

95% CI for mu above to - mu below to: (- 0.013, 0.378)

T-Test mu above to =mu Blow To (vs not =): T = 1.95   P=0.065   DF = 20

Box plots of above and below-town specimens (means are indicated by solid circles)

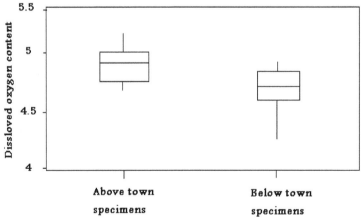

a. Do the data provide sufficient evidence to indicate a difference in mean oxygen content between locations above and below town? Use $\alpha = 0.05$

b. Was the pooled t test or the separate variance t test used in the computer output?

c. Do the required conditions to use the test in (a) appear to be valid for this study? Justify your answer.

d. How large is the difference between the mean oxygen content above and below the town?

First, in variable view the name of variables are entered and in measure part the measure of town is adjusted in nominal (Figure 21). Since, as it mentioned before, nominal data is in categories and cannot be ranked. Here the town is divided in two categories. For town, two values should be described. For doing this, we click on the button in the related cell and define the values for town. Here, we describe two values. This is because we have two places (above town, below town).For above town number one is specified and for below town number two is given (Figures 21 &22). Then, in data view mode the data is entered (Figure 23). Next, the following process should be done.

From the toolbar select Analyze and,

Analyze ⇨ compare means ⇨ independent sample t test

In the independent sample t test window, oxygen is shifted to test variable and town is moved to grouping variable part. Arrow buttons are used to shifting the mentioned variables. For defining the groups, we click on define groups button and for group 1, the number one and for group 2, number two is allocated(Figures 25 & 26) .Finally, press the continue and ok buttons respectively and get the output. The process is shown in pictures below.

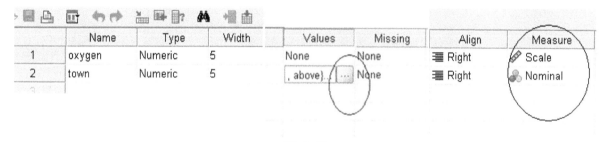

Figure 21

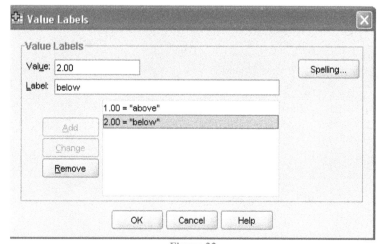

Figure 22

	oxygen	town
1	5.20	1.00
2	4.80	1.00
3	5.10	1.00
4	5.00	1.00
5	4.90	1.00
12	5.10	1.00
13	5.00	1.00
14	4.90	1.00
15	4.90	1.00
16	4.20	2.00
17	4.40	2.00
25	4.30	2.00
26	5.50	2.00
27	4.70	2.00
28	4.90	2.00
29	4.80	2.00
30	4.70	2.00
31		

Figure 23

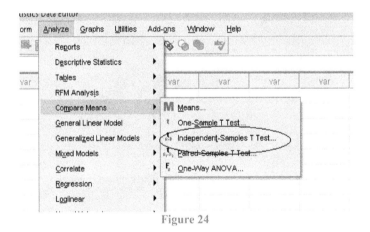

Figure 24

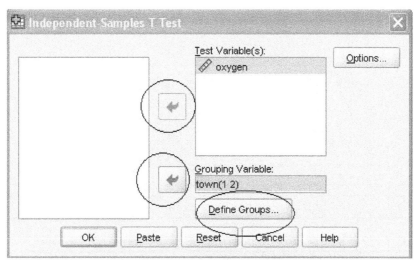

Figure 25

Figure 26

Output is as follows.

Group Statistics

	town	N	Mean	Std. Deviation	Std. Error Mean
oxygen	above	15	4.9200	.15675	.04047
	below	15	4.7400	.32027	.08269

		Levene's Test for Equality of Variances	
		F	Sig.
oxygen	Equal variances assumed	2.893	.100
	Equal variances not assumed		

Steps:

1. H0: $\sigma_1^2 = \sigma_2^2$

   H1: $\sigma_1^2 \neq \sigma_2^2$

P-value = 0.1

Since p-value > α (0.05), we do not reject H0 and conclude variances are equal.

t-test for Equality of Means						
					95% Confidence Interval of the Difference	
t	df	Sig. (2-tailed)	Mean Difference	Std. Error Difference	Lower	Upper
1.955	28	.061	.18000	.09207	-.00859	.36859
1.955	20.343	.064	.18000	.09207	-.01184	.37184

2.

H0: μ above = μ below

H1: μ above ≠ μ below

From the table p-value which is located in first row (0.061) is chosen for investigation. Since, we didn't reject the H0 in first step.

P-value=0.061

Since p-value >α , we do not reject H0 and conclude that oxygen levels above town and below town are not significantly different.

*NOTICE:

*Here we do not divide the 0.061 by 2.Since, the test is two tailed test.

*In statistics we always suppose which null hypothesis is correct .So, the only thing which we do is rejecting it or not.

Example 3-9:

Azuwa, a PhD student, is interested in studying the impact the prior industry experience of the entrepreneurs has on the venture performance. She classified the entrepreneurs into two categories: (1) with prior experience of at least five years and (2) with prior experience of less than five years. She chose nine entrepreneurs from each category running similar size companies. She computed the average profit over the last three years for each company and recorded as follows: (profits are given in 000)

With Exp	88	106	95	118	102	120	86	102	127
Without Exp	92	101	105	130	98	89	100	103	98

a) Describe the data

b) Test if the profits of firms run by entrepreneurs with experience and without experience are greater than the threshold level of 100

c) Azuwa postulates that the average profits of companies run by entrepreneurs with and without experience are different. Test the postulation.

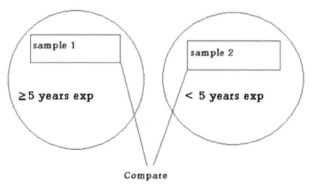

Compare

R.Hashemian 2010- 18

Let μ_{with} be the average profit of companies which is run by entrepreneurs and they have at least 5 years of experience.

Let $\mu_{without}$ be the average profit of companies which is run by entrepreneurs and their experience is less than 5 years.

In this question, there are two variables (profit and experience) .First, experience and profit are entered in variable view mode .Then, two values are described for experience (With and Without).Describing the two values can be done according the process which was being followed in previous question. In column measure in variable view mode, Profit is adjusted in scale mode and experience is considered as nominal.

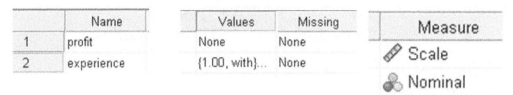

Figure 27

*NOTICE: The amount of profit can be any numerical value. So, it is adjusted in scale mode. However, experience is categorized in two groups.

	profit	experience
1	88.00	1.00
2	106.00	1.00
3	95.00	1.00
4	118.00	1.00

After entering the data in data view, following process is hired.

28 Figure

Analyze ⇨ compare means ⇨ independent sample t test

In the independent sample t test window, profit is shifted to test variable and experience is moved to grouping variable.

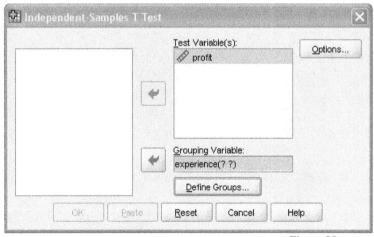

Figure 29

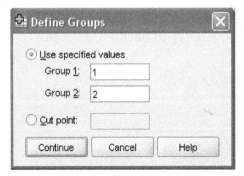

Figure 30

Then, in define groups window , number 1 is entered in group one and number 2 is entered in group two.
Finally, we click continue and ok button and get the output.

Group Statistics

	experience	N	Mean	Std. Deviation	Std. Error Mean
profit	with	9	104.8889	14.34786	4.78262
	without	9	101.7778	11.72367	3.90789

		Levene's Test for Equality of Variances	
		F	Sig.
profit	Equal variances assumed	1.144	.301
	Equal variances not assumed		

First variances are tested .Next, means are tested.

1.

$H_0 : \sigma^2_{with} = \sigma^2_{without}$
$H_1 : \sigma^2_{with} \neq \sigma^2_{without}$
Since p-value $0.301 > 0.05 \Rightarrow$ we do not reject H0.Thus, we conclude variances are equal.
$\sigma^2_{with} = \sigma^2_{without} \Rightarrow$ Thus, the information which is located in first row should be used for comparing the means.

		t-test for Equality of Means					95% Confidence Interval of the Difference	
		t	df	Sig. (2-tailed)	Mean Difference	Std. Error Difference	Lower	Upper
profit		.504	16	.621	3.11111	6.17617	-9.98178	16.20400
		.504	15.389	.622	3.11111	6.17617	-10.02417	16.24639

2.

$H_0 : \sigma^2_{with} = \sigma^2_{without}$
$H_1 : \sigma^2_{with} \neq \sigma^2_{without}$

Since, p-value=0.621>0.05 ⇨ we do not reject H0 .Therefore, we conclude that the average profit of companies which is run by experienced entrepreneurs and without experience ones are not different.

Report:

H1: The average profit of companies which is run by experienced entrepreneurs and without experience ones are different.

To test the above hypothesis, we ran independent sample t test. Based on the results (t=0.504, p-value=0.621).We conclude that hypothesis is not supported. This implies that the average profits that are run by two groups of entrepreneurs are same.

Paired sample t test:

9 -G.Mixner 1998

In this test sample elements which are used in two stages (after and before) are same. Thus, paired sample t test must be used. Two observations are transformed to a single observation by calculating the difference.

(Before – After or After – Before)

n	Before	After	Before - After	After - Before
1	10	12	-2	2
2	15	13	2	-2
3	18	18	0	0

Example 4-9:

After strip mining for coal , the mining company is required to restore the land to its condition prior to mining. One of the many factors considered is the PH of the soil. The area was divided into grids before the mining took place. Fifteen grids were randomly selected and the PH measured. After mining, the PH was measured on the same 15 grids.

The readings are as follows:

Be	100	102	97	100	99	101	101
108	105	104	109	109	99	105	103
Af	102	102	101	107	103	101	108
103	107	101	106	111	104	109	103

a) Has the PH changed significicantly after mining?

a) What does the 95% confidence interval on the difference reveal?

Let Be denotes the reading of PH before mining.

Let AF denotes the reading the PH after mining.

Let δ denotes the difference (Be – Af).

Let μ_σ denotes the average change in PH.

$H_0 : \mu_{\sigma=0}$

$H_1 : \mu_{\sigma \neq 0}$

	BEph	AFph
1	100.00	102.00
2	102.00	102.00
3	97.00	101.00
13	99.00	104.00
14	105.00	109.00
15	103.00	103.00

There are two variables (PH before and PH after).First name of these variables are entered in variable view mode and in measure column both variables are adjusted in scale mode. Then, in data view mode the data for each one is entered.

Figure31

*NOTICE: If the question was, test if Ph has been increased after mining or not. The hypothesis would be such as followings.

If δ =before – after (H1: $\mu_\sigma < 0$), If δ =after – before (H1: $\mu_\sigma > 0$)

Continues,

Next, we follow the process below.

Analyze ⇨ Compare means ⇨ paired sample t test

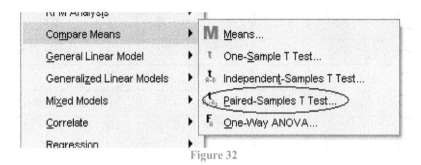

Figure 32

Then, in paired sample t test's window, variables are moved to right side.

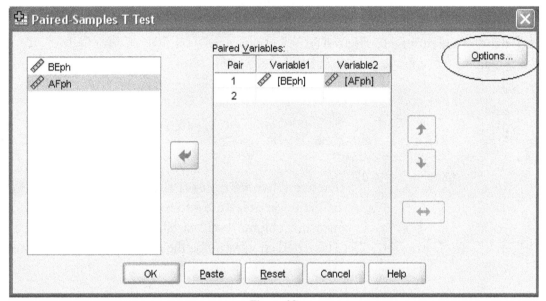

Figure 33

Finally, the ok buttons is pressed and get the output.
We get three tables.

Paired Samples Statistics

		Mean	N	Std. Deviation	Std. Error Mean
Pair 1	BEph	102.8000	15	3.78342	.97688
	AFph	104.5333	15	3.22638	.83305

Paired Samples Correlations

		N	Correlation	Sig.
Pair 1	BEph & AFph	15	.483	.068

Paired Samples Test

		Paired Differences					t	df	Sig. (2-tailed)
		Mean	Std. Deviation	Std. Error Mean	95% Confidence Interval of the Difference				
					Lower	Upper			
Pair 1	BEph - AFph	-1.73333	3.59497	.92822	-3.72416	.25749	-1.867	14	.083

From the third table is revealed which p-value is 0.083.

Since p-value = 0.083 > 0.05 ⇨ we do not reject H (0). Thus, we conclude that the   PH value before and after mining has not significantly been changed.

Report:

H1: The PH of the soil before and after mining is different.

We tested the above hypothesis using paired sample t test. Based on the results (t-value:-1.867, p-value: 0.083).We conclude that the hypothesis is not supported. This implies that PH of soil before and after mining has not been changed significantly.

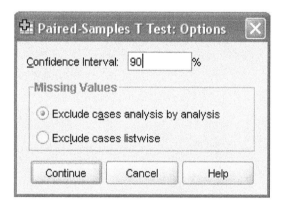

34 Figure

* NOTICE:

During the mentioned process above, CI (confidence interval) can be changed from options (Figures 33 & 34) .As a default, CI has been adjusted in 95%. For example, if we wanted to follow the mentioned test with ∝=0.1(Instead of α= 0.05), the confidence level must be changed to 90%. This can be done from options button.

*90%⇨ ∝=0.1 , 95%⇨ ∝=0.05

So, in ∝=0.1 the following results will be got.

Paired Samples Test

		Paired Differences					t	df	Sig. (2-tailed)
		Mean	Std. Deviation	Std. Error Mean	90% Confidence Interval of the Difference				
					Lower	Upper			
Pair 1	BEph - AFph	-1.73333	3.59497	.92822	-3.36821	-.09845	-1.867	14	.083

P-value=0.083 < 0.1 $\Rightarrow$ H_0 is rejected.
* If 95% CI $\Rightarrow$ LCL= - 3.72, UCL= + 0.2574
(95% CI shows that, the zero value lies between LCL and UCL. There are values below and above zero. This can be the possible reason for rejecting H_0 .)
- If 90% CI $\Rightarrow$ LCL= - 3.36, UCL= - 0.098

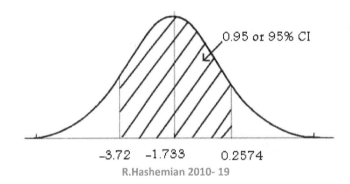

R.Hashemian 2010- 19

Chapter 10: Anova or Analysis of Variance

What is Anova or Analysis of Variance?

This test is used for testing more than two sample means as well as in the case of having more than two samples, this test can be used.

There are two types of anova: One way and two ways.

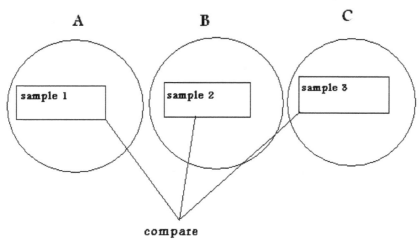

R.Hashemian 2010- 20

For instance, we have three samples A, B, C and their means are μ A, μ B and μ C respectively:

Let μ A denotes the mean of population A.
Let μ B denotes the mean of population B.
Let μ C denotes the mean of population C.

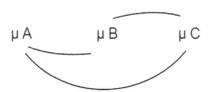

The maximum amount of first type error is showed by α-value. Let, compare the means two by two and see what is happening for α-value.

μ A, μ B 1-0.05=0.95
μ A, μ C 1-0.05=0.95
} ⟶ 1-(0.95*0.95) = 1- 0.9025=0.0975

As it is revealed from above, 0.0975 is much bigger than 0.05.

Here the point is, if we will compare means, what is the relationship between anova and analysis of variances?

For better understanding follow the example below.

	Experiment 1			Experiment 2		
	Sample1	Sample2	Sample3	Sample1	Sample2	Sample3
	4.9	5.4	5.9	4.5	5	5.5
	5.1	5.6	6.1	5.5	6	6.5
	5	5.5	6	5	5.5	6
	5.2	5.3	6.2	4	4.5	5
	4.8	5.7	5.8	6	6.5	7
Mean	5	5.5	6	5	5.5	6

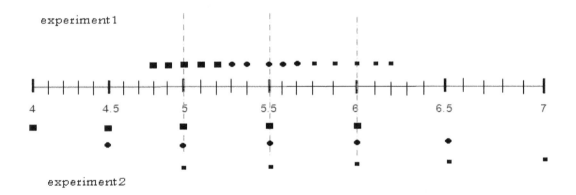

R.Hashemian 2010- 21

As it can be seen from illustration above and in experiment 1, overlap among samples does not exist as well as variance inside samples is low. However, in experiment 2 there is huge overlap among samples and variance inside samples is high.

Variance can be between samples or within samples.

If between samples variance > within sample variance ⇨ Means are different
If between samples variance < within sample variance ⇨ means are not different
Thus, in experiment 1, means are different .However; in experiment 2 means are not different. Even though, 5.0, 5.5 and 6 are different mathematically. However, these numbers in experiment 2 statistically are not different.

Example1-10 :

Anusuiya, PhD student is interested in studying the nicotine content of four different brands of cigarettes (A, B, C and D). Within the same brand nicotine content varies. Anusuiya wants to test if the nicotine content across the brands is different. She buys 10 cigarettes from each brand and tests for the nicotine content. The observations are as follows:

Brand A	10.07	9.47	9.12	11.37	11.40
11.29	10.68	8.13	10.51	10.66	
Brand B	8.60	8.13	11.34	9.35	9.30
10.02	9.58	6.46	8.26	5.01	
Brand C	6.79	10.92	11.39	9.70	8.04
10.72	11.24	7.71	7.57	9.09	
Brand D	9.96	5.85	10.30	9.71	10.75
8.03	13.13	11.86	11.33	10.48	

a. Help Anusuiya test her hypothesis
b.Find the brands that have different nicotine content.
c.If you use independent samples t test to test the above hypothesis, how many pair wise comparisons are required? Why is it not advisable to test pair wise?

Let μ A denotes the average nicotine content of brand A.
Let μ B denotes the average nicotine content of brand B.
Let μ C denotes the average nicotine content of brand C.
Let μ D denotes the average nicotine content of brand D.

H0: $\mu A=\mu B=\mu C=\mu D$
H1: At least one of them is different.

The variables and data should be entered as follows.
The name of two variables should be entered in variable view mode in column name. The measure of brand and nicotine content are nominal and scale respectively.

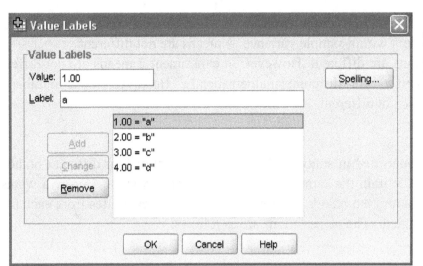

For brand and in value column, four labels should be described.

35 Figure

	nicotineconte nt	brand
1	10.07	1.00
2	9.47	1.00
11	8.60	2.00
12	8.13	2.00
21	6.79	3.00
22	10.92	3.00
39	11.33	4.00
40	10.48	4.00

Then, data is entered in data view mode.
Next the following process is done.
 Analyze ⇨ Compare means ⇨ one way anova

36 Figure

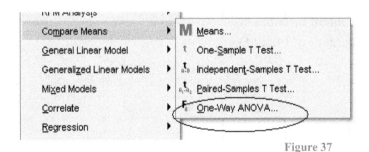

Figure 37

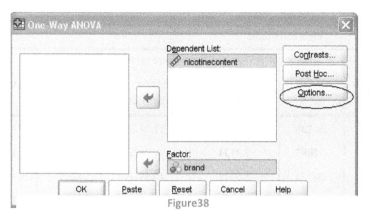
Figure38

After executing the one way anova, the one way anova window is appeared. In mentioned window nicotine content is shifted to dependent list as well as brand is moved to factor.

With click on **options** button, the related window is opened. Descriptive and means plot (for drawing the graph) are signed and press continue and ok buttons.

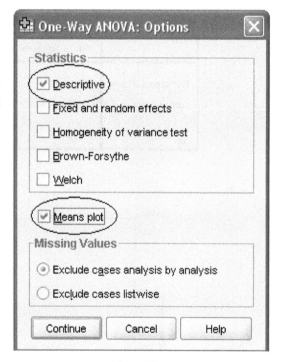
Figure39

Finally, the output is got.

Descriptives

nicotinecontent

	N	Mean	Std. Deviation	Std. Error	95% Confidence Interval for Mean		Minimum	Maximum
					Lower Bound	Upper Bound		
a	10	10.2700	1.07946	.34136	9.4978	11.0422	8.13	11.40
b	10	8.6050	1.80557	.57097	7.3134	9.8966	5.01	11.34
c	10	9.3170	1.71213	.54142	8.0922	10.5418	6.79	11.39
d	10	10.1400	2.02488	.64032	8.6915	11.5885	5.85	13.13
Total	40	9.5830	1.76291	.27874	9.0192	10.1468	5.01	13.13

ANOVA

nicotine content

	Sum of Squares	df	Mean Square	F	Sig.
Between Groups	18.095	3	6.032	2.106	.117
Within Groups	103.112	36	2.864		
Total	121.206	39			

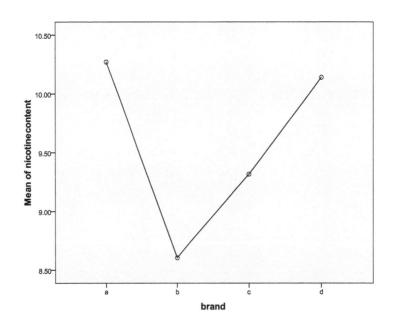

P-value=0.117,
Since p-value > α, we do not reject the null hypothesis. We conclude that the mean nicotine content of 4 brands is same.If Confidence intervals were being compared for 4 brands and regarding lower and upper points, the overlap in many parts can be seen. Thus, we conclude that their means are not in that much different.

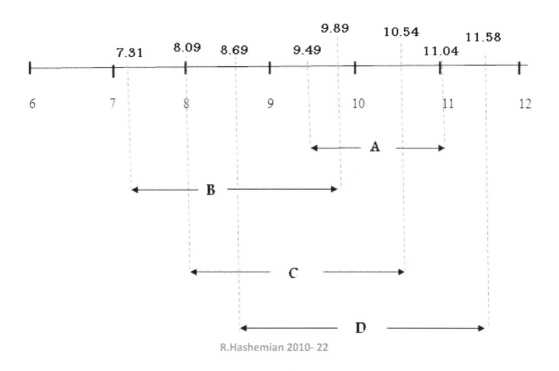

R.Hashemian 2010- 22

Report:

H1: Mean nicotine contents of four brands are different.
We performed one way anova to test the hypothesis .Based on the test results (f-value= 2.106, P-value=0.117), we do not support the hypothesis. This implies that the mean nicotine content of four brands (A, B, C, D) are same.

Now, we are going to add the number 2 to data of brand A and test the data again. For adding the number 2 to data, we create a new variable and we call it **new nicotine**. For doing the mentioned process, we hire the **transform** from toolbar.

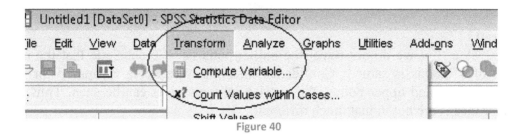

Figure 40

Transform ⇨ compute variable

In compute variable mode , type the new variables' name in target variable and arrow button is used to shift the nicotine content to numeric expression .Mathematic tools below the numeric expression part are used for adding number two to nicotine content. Then, IF button is hired for describing the circumstances of the process.

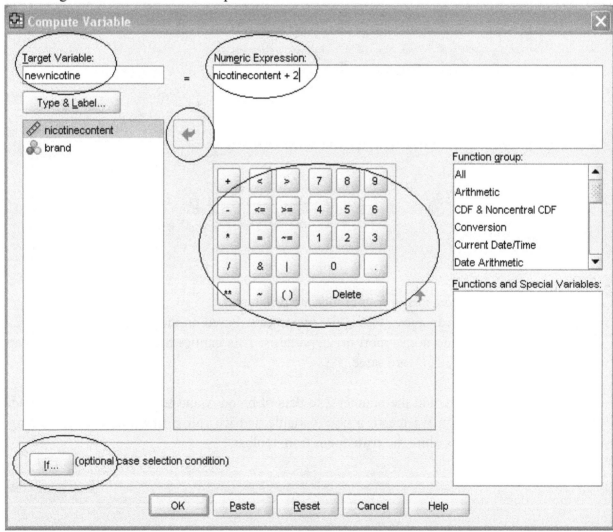

Figure 41

Since, we would like to add the number 2 to brand A. In addition, brand A was given label one at the beginning of the process (in variable view mode).Thus, in **COMPUTE VARIABELS: IF CASES** window, brand is shifted to right side and it is equaled to one.

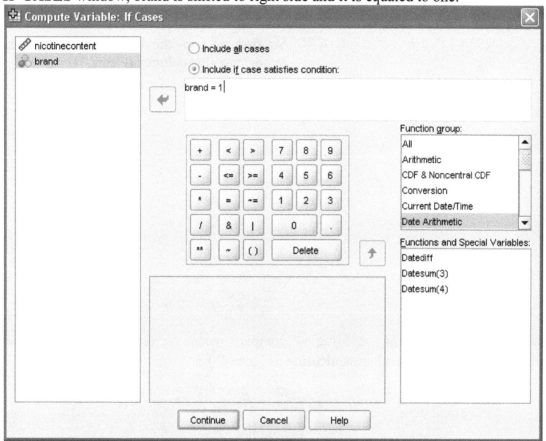

Figure 42

	nicotineconte nt	brand	newnicotine
1	10.07	1.00	12.07
2	9.47	1.00	11.47
3	9.12	1.00	11.12
4	11.37	1.00	13.37
5	11.40	1.00	13.40
6	11.29	1.00	13.29
7	10.68	1.00	12.68
8	8.13	1.00	10.13
9	10.51	1.00	12.51
10	10.66	1.00	12.66
11	8.60	2.00	.
12	8.13	2.00	.

Finally, press the continue and ok buttons. As a result, a new variable (new nicotine) is added to our SPSS table. And it's data is equal to the data of brand A plus 2.
(Figure 43)

43 Figure

Let do the Anova one way again. However, this time the data for brand A has been changed. This is because; we are going to use the new nicotine instead of nicotine content.

	nicotinecontent	brand	newnicotine
1	10.07	1.00	12.07
9	10.51	1.00	12.51
10	10.66	1.00	12.66
11	8.60	2.00	8.60
12	8.13	2.00	8.13
13	11.34	2.00	11.34
21	6.79	3.00	6.79
22	10.92	3.00	10.92
23	11.39	3.00	11.39
38	11.86	4.00	11.86
39	11.33	4.00	11.33
40	10.48	4.00	10.48

So, first, we copy the data of brands B, C and D to new nicotine column. (Figure 44)

44 Figure

And follow the same process. (Analyze ⇨ compare means ⇨ one way anova).However, **nicotine content** is replaced with **new nicotine**. (Figure 45).

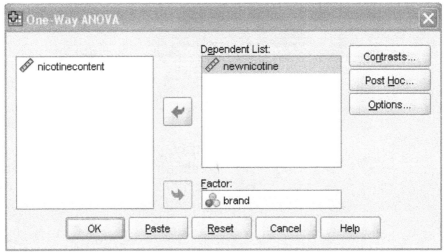

Figure 45

Then, click the ok. However, this time the value which is got for p-value is different from previous time.

ANOVA

new nicotine

	Sum of Squares	df	Mean Square	F	Sig.
Between Groups	75.575	3	25.192	8.795	.000
Within Groups	103.112	36	2.864		
Total	178.686	39			

P-value → 0.000.Since, 0.000 < 0.05, we reject H0.

While performing the Anova to test equality of means, if null hypothesis is rejected, perform the **post-hoc test**. Basic purpose of post hoc test is to compare means and identify the means that are different and that are not different.

For doing the post hoc, we follow the below process.

Analyze ⇨ compare means ⇨ one way anova ⇨ post hoc test

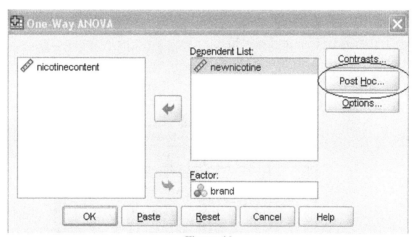

Figure 46

If the samples sizes were same, in post hoc mode we will sign the **tukeys-b.** Otherwise, **S-N-K test** must be signed. We will sign the tukeys-b. Since, the numbers of samples for all brands are same.

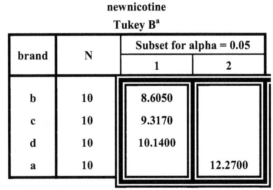

Figure 47

Finally, we press the ok button and get the output.

newnicotine

Tukey B[a]

brand	N	Subset for alpha = 0.05	
		1	2
b	10	8.6050	
c	10	9.3170	
d	10	10.1400	
a	10		12.2700

Means for groups in homogeneous subsets are
displayed.

a. Uses Harmonic Mean Sample Size = 10.000.

Report:

H1: Mean nicotine content of four brands (A,B,C,D) are different. We performed one way anova to test the hypothesis. Based on the test results (F-value= 8.795, P-value= 0.00).We support the hypothesis H1.This implies that the mean nicotine content of four brands are different. In order to compare the brands whose nicotine content is different, we performed post hoc test using TUKEYS HSD.

Based on the results we conclude:

- Mean nicotine content of brands B,C and D are same.

- Mean nicotine content of brand A is different from the mean nicotine content of brands B, C and D.

Let add number 2 to brand D (4).In this case we follow the same process. However, the number 1(Brand A) will be replaced with number 4(Brand D). (Figure 48)

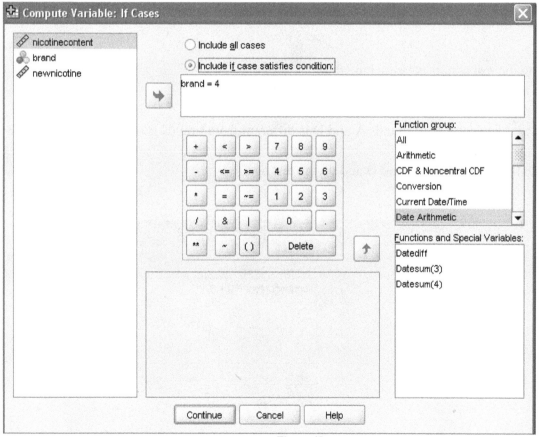

Figure 48

The amount of p-value will be 0.000.So; we reject the H0 and do the post hoc test. We sign the tukeys-b. Since, numbers of samples are same. Finally, we get the output.

newnicotine

Tukey B[a]

brand	N	Subset for alpha = 0.05	
		1	2
b	10	8.6050	
c	10	9.3170	
d	10		12.1400
a	10		12.2700

Means for groups in homogeneous subsets are
displayed.

a. Uses Harmonic Mean Sample Size = 10.000.

Based on the test results we conclude that:
- Mean nicotine content of brands B and C are same.
- Mean nicotine content of brand A and D are same.
- Mean nicotine content of brands A and D is different from brands B and C.

Let add another 3 units to brand D and do the test again.

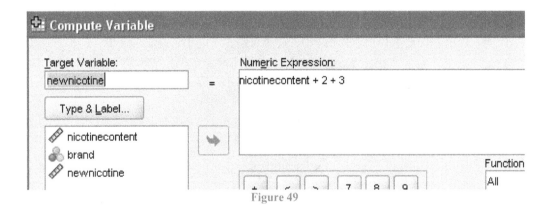

Figure 49

The gotten output is as follows.

newnicotine

Tukey B[a]

brand	N	Subset for alpha = 0.05		
		1	2	3
b	10	8.6050		
c	10	9.3170		
a	10		12.2700	
d	10			15.1400

Means for groups in homogeneous subsets are displayed.

a. Uses Harmonic Mean Sample Size = 10.000.

Based on post hoc test results we conclude that:

- Mean nicotine content of brands B and C are same.
- Mean nicotine content of brands B and C is different from mean nicotine content of brands A and D.
- Mean nicotine content of brand A is different from mean nicotine content of brand D.

We can use some statements such as, lower or higher instead of phrase different from.

Let answer to part C of the question.(If you use independent samples t test to test the above hypothesis, how many pair wise comparisons are required? Why is it not advisable to test pair wise?)

6	A	B	C	D
A		*	*	*
B			*	*
C				*
D				

As it can be seen from the table, there are 6 possibilities. If we wanted to use independent sample t test, CI would not be 95% and $\alpha = 1-(0.95)$ is much more than 0.05.

*NOTICE:

For calculating variability among data, coefficient of variation should be used and it is calculated from following formulas.

$$\frac{\text{standard deviation of population}(\sigma)}{\text{mean of population } (\mu)} , \frac{\text{standard deviation of sample}(s)}{\text{mean of sample } (\bar{x})}$$

Example 2-10: A-10/50=0.2, B-30/200=0.15, in this example 30 is bigger than 10.However; variability in A is more than B.

Chapter 11: Test for Normality

What is Normality Test?

Up to this part we have supposed which all samples that have been used for tests have had normal distribution. However, in reality the normality of samples must be tested. It is testing if the data for a variable of interest comes from a normal distribution or not. When we perform one sample test or two sample test or ANOVA, we do the normality test. We make use of "t" distribution (one sample/two sample) and "F" distribution (anova).These distributions are sensitive to normality assumption.

Two major tests for testing the normality:
1. Chi-square test
2. Kolmogorov-smirnav (k-s) test

We are going to discuss about the **K-S test**.
K-S test is used widely by many statistical packages to test for normality because the test is robust and gives accurate results.
Our hypothesis for testing normality will be as follows.

H0: the data comes from a normal distribution
H1: the data does not come from a normal distribution

In fact, K-S test compares the observed values (real data) with expected values (data when the distribution is normal).

Example 1-11:

Stephanie, a PhD student, is studying the impact of organizational policies on job commitment and job satisfaction of employees. She conducts a pilot study with 15 employees in a company. She has designed the questionnaire based on items from previous studies. Each construct (job commitment and job satisfaction) has six items and each item is scored using a 5-type Likert-scale (5-strongly agree and 1-strongly disagree).
A higher score indicates high levels of commitment/satisfaction. The job commitment (JS) scores of 15 employees are given as follows:

JC	20	23	27	26	19	17	21	22	24
25	15	19	20	22	24				
JS	18	24	27	20	22	20	24	21	24
25	20	15	17	20	22				

a) Test if the average scores of JC and JS are greater than 21
b) Which score has more variability? Explain.

	jc	js
1	20.00	18.00
2	23.00	24.00
3	27.00	27.00
4	26.00	20.00
5	19.00	22.00
6	17.00	20.00
7	21.00	24.00
8	22.00	21.00
9	24.00	24.00
10	25.00	25.00
11	15.00	20.00
12	19.00	15.00
13	20.00	17.00
14	22.00	20.00
15	24.00	22.00

50 Figure

In this question we would like to test the normality of JC .After entering the data, for performing the test the following process is hired.

Analyze ⇨ Non parametric tests ⇨ 1-sample k-s

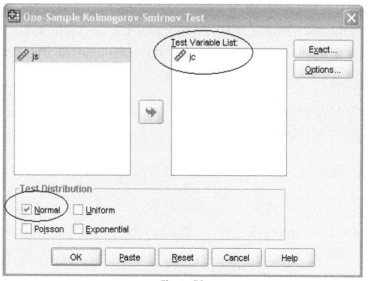

Figure 51

In k-s test, we move theJC to test variable list. Since, we would like to test the normality of data for JC. The **normal** should be signed. Then press the ok button.

One-Sample Kolmogorov-Smirnov Test

		jc
N		15
Normal Parameters[a,b]	Mean	21.6000
	Std. Deviation	3.35517
Most Extreme Differences	Absolute	.096
	Positive	.083
	Negative	-.096
Kolmogorov-Smirnov Z		.372
Asymp. Sig. (2-tailed)		.999

a. Test distribution is Normal.

b. Calculated from data.

-This test always is 2-tailed.

Report:

We tested for normality using k-s test, because on the results (K-S Z=0.37, p-value=0.999) the data comes from the normal distribution.

Review:

Step 1:

H0: the data comes from a normal distribution

H1: the data does not come from a normal distribution

*NOTICE:

We don't know if the distribution of JC is normal or not. In addition we use nonparametric test. Regarding what was mentioned and the definition of Nonparametric, the hypothesis will be as above.

Step 2:

$\alpha = 0.05$, K-S Z =0.372, p-value=0.999

Since p-value > α, we do not reject H0.

Step 3:

We conclude that the data comes from a normal distribution.

Example 2-11:

Fook, PhD student, is interested in studying the impact of Gender on EI (Emotional Intelligence)at Nestle Malaysia. The female/male employees are in ratio of 3:2.He took a sample of 15 female employees and 10 male employees and calculated their EI levels. EI score is calculated on a standardized scale of 150.The data collected by Fook are as follows:

F	88	106	95	118	102	120	86	102	78	127
108	89	85	102	100						
M	92	101	105	130	98	89	100	93	103	83

a) Test if individual average EIs are greater than the threshold level of 100
b) Fook postulates that female's average EI is greater than the average EI of males. Test Fook's postulation.

	female	male
1	88.00	92.00
2	106.00	101.00
3	95.00	105.00
4	118.00	130.00
5	102.00	98.00
6	120.00	89.00
7	86.00	100.00
8	102.00	93.00
9	78.00	103.00
10	127.00	83.00
11	108.00	.
12	89.00	.
13	85.00	.
14	102.00	.
15	100.00	.

52 Figure

In this question we try to test the normality of data for female. After entering the data, the normality test is done similar to previous question.

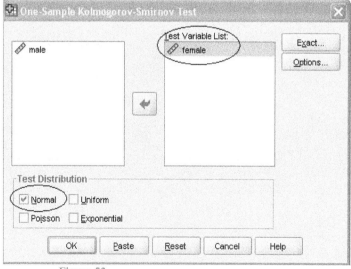

Figure 53

The output is as follows.

One-Sample Kolmogorov-Smirnov Test

		female
N		15
Normal Parameters[a,b]	Mean	100.4000
	Std. Deviation	14.03465
Most Extreme Differences	Absolute	.125
	Positive	.125
	Negative	-.095
Kolmogorov-Smirnov Z		.484
Asymp. Sig. (2-tailed)		.973

a. Test distribution is Normal.

b. Calculated from data.

H0: the data comes from a normal distribution.

H1: the data does not come from a normal distribution.

K-S Z= 0.484, P-value = 0.97 > 0.05 ➜ Thus, data for female has normal distribution.

Chapter 12: Correlation and Regression

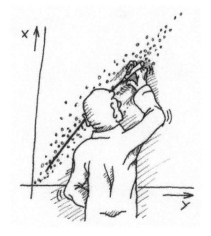

Correlation and Regression are appropriate tools to study relationship between the variables and they show how one variable behaves with respect to the behavior of another variable. Furthermore, they can be used for forecasting as well as predicting of the behavior of a variable.

10 -G.Mixner 1998

Independent and dependant variables
In previous chapters the nature of dependent and independent variables were explained.
*NOTICE: Behavior of the dependant variable is determined by the behavior of independent variables.

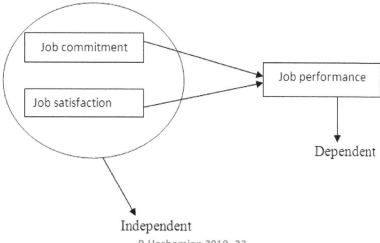

R.Hashemian 2010- 23

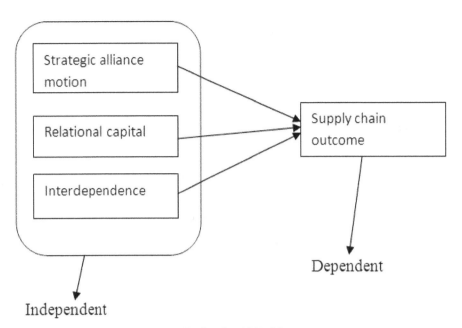

R.Hashemian 2010- 24

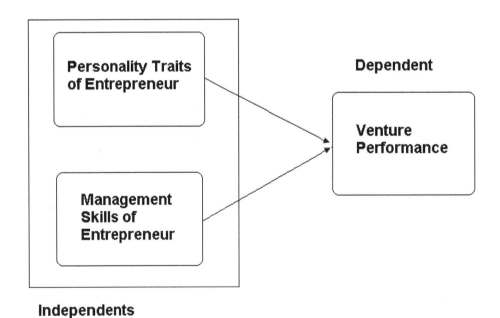

R.Hashemian 2010- 25

Different kinds of relationships between variables:

Different kinds of relationships between variables are shown in graphs below.

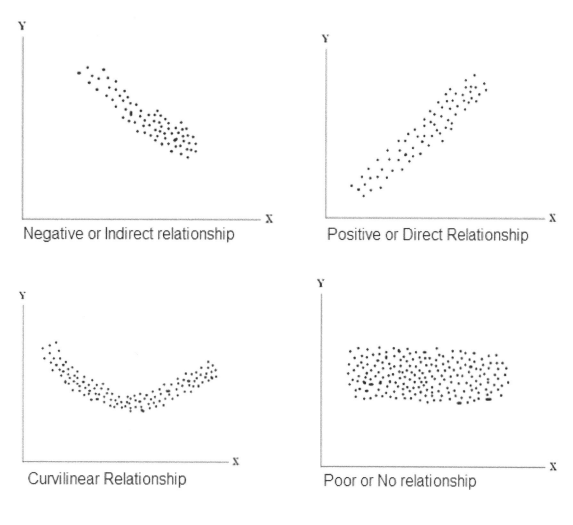

R.Hashemian 2010- 26

-In positive or direct relationship with increase in x, y is increased as well.

-In negative or indirect relationship with increase in x, y is decreased.

-In positive and negative relationships, the relationship between x and y is linear.

-In curvilinear the relationship between x and y is quadratic curve and it's equation is as follows.

$$Y = ax^2 + bx + c$$

-In poor relationship, there is not any relationship among variables or the relationship is so weak.

Regression

In regression,

-historical data will be our base

-we assume that the relationship between independent and dependent variable is linear.

-we assume the conditions existed in the past will be true in the future. This enables us to predict the,

*Relationship between dependent and independent variables.

*Value of the dependent variable based on the levels of independent variables.

-Regression does not guarantee cause and effect relationships.

*NOTICE: There are two kinds of study: A. longitudinal study B. Cross sectional study.

In linear regression the equation is as follows which shows the relationship between dependent and independent variables.

$Y = a + b1 x1 + b2 x2 + \ldots\ldots + e$

a is constant and b shows the slope of the graph. Both a and b are called parameters of regression equation (Also called coefficients).

Y is dependent variable and x is independent variable.

e stands for error.

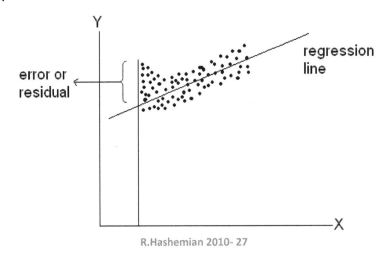

R.Hashemian 2010- 27

The difference between actual value and value of regression is called error.

Number of independent variable	Number of dependent variable	Different types of regression
one	one	Simple regression
More than one	one	Multiple regression

Bivariate Data Analysis:

It is hired when data analysis and hypothesis testing is involved with investigation of the association or differences between two variables simultaneously.

1 G. Meixner 1998

Example1-12:

A doctor has the following data about his 10 heart patients. He wants to study the factors that influence congestive heart failures. The doctor has characterized heart failures using cardiac index.

Age(years)	Disease duration(years)	Weight	Cardiac Index
67	5	57	1.6
45	2	67	2.4
59	8	102	2.2
63	1	75	1.7
55	1	92	2.3
65	1	90	1.6
62	2	67	1.4
60	1	72	2.2
72	2	71	1.3
44	0.25	68	2.4

a. Identify the factors that influence cardiac index (assume that each variable follows a normal distribution) and interpret the results.

b. the doctor feels that weight and age maybe correlated to disease duration. Test the intuition of the doctor using correlation and co linearity diagnostics.

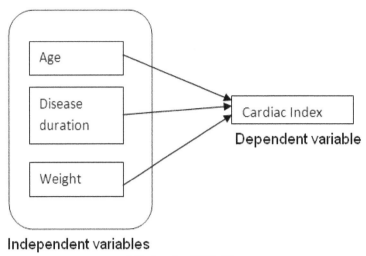

Dependent variable

Independent variables

R.Hashemian 2010- 28

The multiple regression must be used in this question. This is because the numbers of independent variables are more than one.

First the variables are described in variable view and data is entered in data view.

	age	duration	weight	cardindex
1	67.00	5.00	57.00	1.60
2	45.00	2.00	67.00	2.40
3	59.00	8.00	102.00	2.20
4	63.00	1.00	75.00	1.70
5	55.00	1.00	92.00	2.30
6	65.00	1.00	90.00	1.60
7	62.00	2.00	67.00	1.40
8	60.00	1.00	72.00	2.20
9	72.00	2.00	71.00	1.30
10	44.00	0.25	68.00	2.40

Figure 54

It is better to test the relationship between variables two by two before doing the regression. So, we hire the bivariate test for performing this issue. Thus, the following process should be done.

Analyze ⇨ correlate ⇨ bivariate

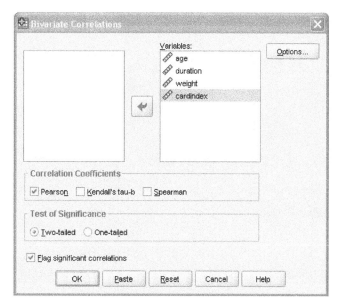

55 Figure

In bivariate correlation window, all the variables are moved to right side. Then, press ok.

*NOTICE:

In correlation:

- Value is between -1 and +1.
- Closer to -1 indicates strong negative relationship.
-Closer to +1 indicates strong positive relationship.
- Closer to zero indicates no or poor relationship.

Finally, we can get the output.

Correlations

		age	duration	weight	cardindex
age	Pearson Correlation	1	.221	.012	-.862[**]
	Sig. (2-tailed)		.540	.973	.001
	N	10	10	10	10
duration	Pearson Correlation	.221	1	.293	-.022
	Sig. (2-tailed)	.540		.412	.951
	N	10	10	10	10
weight	Pearson Correlation	.012	.293	1	.253
	Sig. (2-tailed)	.973	.412		.481
	N	10	10	10	10
cardindex	Pearson Correlation	-.862[**]	-.022	.253	1
	Sig. (2-tailed)	.001	.951	.481	
	N	10	10	10	10

**. Correlation is significant at the 0.01 level (2-tailed).

-Correlation is significant at the 0.01 levels (2-tailed)
In next step we are going to do the regression.

Analyze ⇨ regression ⇨ linear

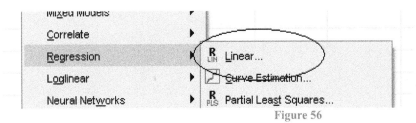

Figure 56

The variables are shifted to their specific places and test is done.(Cardiac Index is Dependent and the rest are Independent)

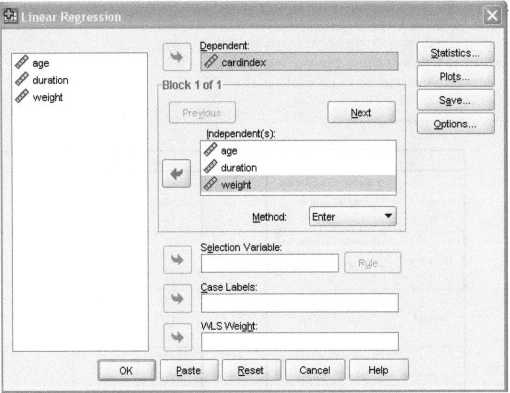

Figure 57

Output is as follows.

Variables Entered/Removed

Model	Variables Entered	Variables Removed	Method
1	weight, age, duration[a]	.	Enter

a. All requested variables entered.

Model Summary

Model	R	R Square	Adjusted R Square	Std. Error of the Estimate
1	.907[a]	.822	.733	.22257

a. Predictors: (Constant), weight, age, duration

ANOVA[b]

Model		Sum of Squares	df	Mean Square	F	Sig.
1	Regression	1.372	3	.457	9.230	.011[a]
	Residual	.297	6	.050		
	Total	1.669	9			

a. Predictors: (Constant), weight, age, duration
b. Dependent Variable: cardindex

Coefficients[a]

Model		Unstandardized Coefficients		Standardized Coefficients	t	Sig.
		B	Std. Error	Beta		
1	(Constant)	3.831	.653		5.862	.001
	age	-.042	.008	-.888	-5.019	.002
	duration	.019	.033	.105	.568	.590
	weight	.007	.006	.233	1.290	.244

a. Dependent Variable: cardindex

In second table from above, R Square is called coefficient of determination. The related number to R Square is used for showing the goodness of regression fit. **R Square always is located between zero and one. If it was closer to one, regression fit is good** and can be used for prediction purpose. On the other hand, closer to zero indicates that regression fit is poor and cannot be used for prediction purpose.

In our example R Square = 82.2% or 0.822.Thus , 82.2 % of the variance (behavior) in the dependent variable (cardiac index) can be explained by the independent variables(Age , Disease duration and weight).So , 17.8 % (100-82.2) is not explainable with independent variables and it is caused by other unknown variables.

In third table the results of anova are observed. We are introducing two hypotheses.

H0: the regression fit is not good.

H1: The regression fit is good.

According the third table f-value = 9.230, p-value = 0.011

Since p-value < α (0.05), we reject H0 and conclude that regression fit is good.

The last table shows the coefficients .The coefficients are placed in related locations in equation and the equation comes as follows.

Y= a + bx

Y= a +b1x1 + b2x2 + … + e

Caindex = 3.831 - 0.042 Age + 0.019 Duration + 0.007 Weight

As it can be seen from last table p-values of independent variables are as follows.

Variable	P-value
Age	0.002
Duration	0.590
Weight	0.244

The following hypotheses are introduced.

H0: Age does not have a significant relationship with caindex.
H1: Age has a significant relationship with caindex.

H0: Duration does not have a significant relationship with caindex
H1: Duration has a significant relationship with caindex

H0: weight does not have a significant relationship with caindex
H1: weight has a significant relationship with caindex

As it can be seen from the p-values belong to the independent variables, only the p-value of age is less than α. (0.002 < 0.005).So, we reject the null hypothesis belong to Age and we conclude that only age has significant relationship with caindex. So, the equation will be as follows.

Caindex=3.831-0.042age

The coefficient's sign of age is negative. Thus, there is a negative relationship between Cardiac Index and Age.

Beta Coefficient or Standardized Coefficient:

Regarding 4th table above , Beta variable or standardized coefficient indicates relative importance of an independent variable in predicting dependent variable. Suppose, all three variables have significant effects on dependent variable. However, the importance of age is more than others. This is because; the amount of beta for Age is more than others (0.888).

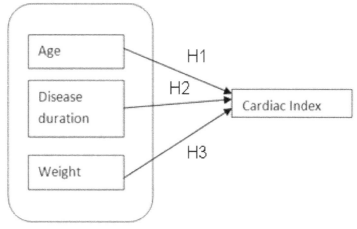

R.Hashemian 2010- 29

Report:

H1: age has a negative relationship with cardiac index
H2: duration has a positive relationship with cardiac index
H3: weight has a positive relationship with cardiac index
We performed multiple regression to test the hypothesis. Based on the test results, we conclude the following:
1) Regression as a whole is significant (F-value=9.230.P-value=0.011) with an R^2 value of 0.822.this implies that 82.2% of the variance in the dependent variable can be explained by the independent variables.

2) Among the independent variables only age is found to have significant negative relationship with cardiac index (t-value=-5.019, p-value=0.002).this implies that as age increases, cardiac index decreases. Of the three hypotheses, only H1 is supported.

Bonus points:

Nowadays, Amos is bundled with SPSS and it is one of the easiest ways to do the path analysis. It's ease is based on the fact that you draw your model in the program.

Amos steps:

   a. Open AMOS
   b. Tell AMOS what SPSS data set to use
   c. Draw your variables in AMOS
   d. Select estimation and output options
   e. Draw your model(s)
   f. Run your model

Chapter 13: Multi-Collinearity effect

What is Multi-collinearity Effect?

When independent variables are strongly correlated with one another, it is difficult to predict the relationship between dependent and independent variables.

Example 1-13:
Refer to example one from chapter 11

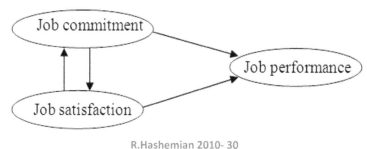

R.Hashemian 2010- 30

In mentioned example Job satisfaction and Job commitment are independent variables and Job performance is dependent variable. However, any relationship between job satisfaction and job commitment causes to Multi-collinearity effect.

Example 2-13:
Refer to example in chapter 12
In this example the existence of any relationship among age, disease duration and weight can cause to Multi-co linearity effect.

	age	duration	weight	cardindex
1	67.00	5.00	57.00	1.60
2	45.00	2.00	67.00	2.40
3	59.00	8.00	102.00	2.20
4	63.00	1.00	75.00	1.70
5	55.00	1.00	92.00	2.30
6	65.00	1.00	90.00	1.60
7	62.00	2.00	67.00	1.40
8	60.00	1.00	72.00	2.20
9	72.00	2.00	71.00	1.30
10	44.00	0.25	68.00	2.40

Figure58

For finding the Multi-collinearity effect, after entering the data, following process is hired.

Analyze ⇨ regression ⇨ linear ⇨ statistics ⇨ sign the collinearity diagnostics
(Cardiac Index is moved to Dependent and the rest are shifted to Independent part.)

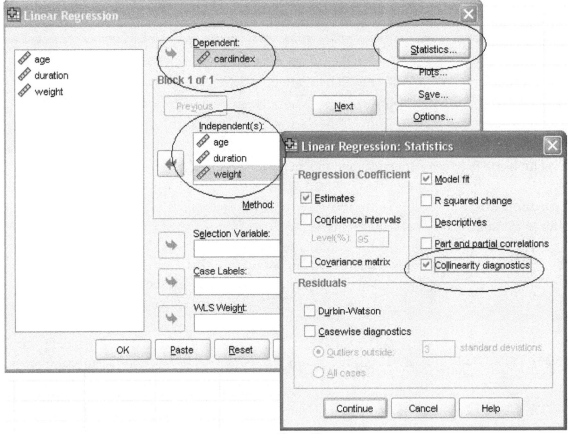

Figure 59

After pressing the ok button the output is got. The 4th table is shown below.

Coefficients[a]

Model		Unstandardized Coefficients		Standardized Coefficients	t	Sig.	Collinearity Statistics	
		B	Std. Error	Beta			Tolerance	VIF
1	(Constant)	3.831	.653		5.862	.001		
	age	-.042	.008	-.888	-5.019	.002	.948	1.054
	duration	.019	.033	.105	.568	.590	.867	1.153
	weight	.007	.006	.233	1.290	.244	.911	1.097

a. Dependent Variable: cardindex

- In the left side column of the table above, VIF stands for Variance Inflation Factor. Tolerance is calculated from the equation below.

$$\text{Tolerance} = \frac{1}{VIF}$$

- If VIF > 5, there is evidence of Multi-co linearity effect.
- In this example all VIFS are less than 5. Thus, there is not any Multi-co linearity effect.

Example 3-13:

Cording, christmann, and king (2008) have studied the integration of firms through acquisition. In particular, they studied the role of market expansion between market focus (independent variable) and acquisition performance (dependent variable). They have postulated that (1) greater the market focus during integration, greater the market expansion and (2) greater the market expansion, the greater the acquisition performance.

a. Identify the role of market expansion (mediator, moderator, or intervening) and draw the framework depicting the role.

Suppose the scores on these three variables are as follows:

trial	1	2	3	4	5	6	7	8	9	10	11	12	13	14	15
MF	18	15	19	22	15	16	17	19	19	20	21	21	18	23	22
AP	39	30	47	56	28	26	26	35	36	42	43	40	38	52	49
ME	16	15	18	21	13	12	13	15	16	17	20	20	16	20	20

MF-Market Focus, AP – Acquisition Performance, ME- Market Expansion
b. Test for the role identified in a.

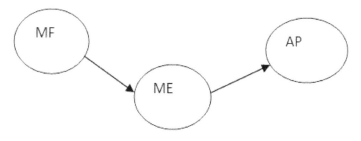

31 -R.Hashemian 2010

In this example ME is mediating variable.
Variable ME is a mediator of the relationship between MF and AP. Since , ME helps explain **how** or **why** MF is related to AP.

	mf	ap	me
1	18.00	39.00	16.00
2	15.00	30.00	15.00
3	19.00	47.00	18.00
4	22.00	56.00	21.00
5	15.00	28.00	13.00
6	16.00	26.00	12.00
7	17.00	26.00	13.00
8	19.00	35.00	15.00
9	19.00	36.00	16.00
10	20.00	42.00	17.00
11	21.00	43.00	20.00
12	21.00	40.00	20.00
13	18.00	38.00	16.00
14	23.00	52.00	20.00
15	22.00	49.00	20.00

60 Figure

First enter the data.
As it was mentioned before, it is better to test the relationship between variables two by two before doing the regression. So, the bivariate test is done.

Analyze ⇨ Correlate ⇨ Bivariate
(Move the **mf,ap,me** to variables part)

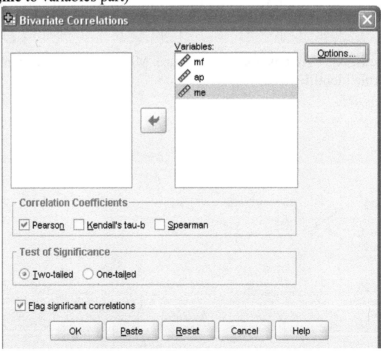

Figure 61

Correlations		mf	ap	me
mf	Pearson Correlation	1	.883**	.903**
	Sig. (2-tailed)		.000	.000
	N	15	15	15
ap	Pearson Correlation	.883**	1	.919**
	Sig. (2-tailed)	.000		.000
	N	15	15	15
me	Pearson Correlation	.903**	.919**	1
	Sig. (2-tailed)	.000	.000	
	N	15	15	15

**. Correlation is significant at the 0.01 level (2-tailed).

The result reveals that, there is a relationship between MF and ME. (If Pearson correlation was closer to 1 or -1, indicates more relationship, either positive or negative)

*NOTICE:
In correlation:
- Value is between -1 and +1.
- Closer to -1 indicates strong negative relationship.
 -Closer to +1 indicates strong positive relationship.
- Closer to zero indicates no or poor relationship.

Then, Analyze ⇨ regression ⇨ linear ⇨ statistics ⇨ sign the collinearity diagnostics. (ap is dependent and me, mf are considered as independents.)

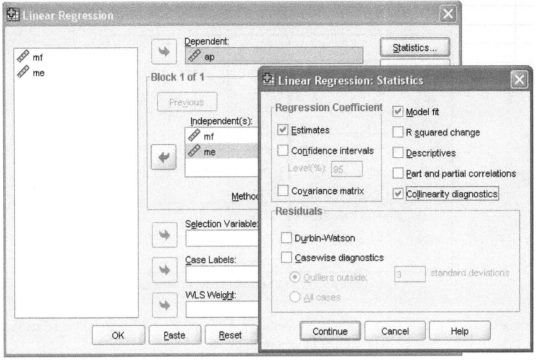

Figure 62

Press the ok and get the output.

Variables Entered/Removed

Model	Variables Entered	Variables Removed	Method
1	me, mf[a]	.	Enter

a. All requested variables entered.

Model Summary

Model	R	R Square	Adjusted R Square	Std. Error of the Estimate
1	.928[a]	.860	.837	3.75699

a. Predictors: (Constant), me, mf

ANOVA[b]

Model		Sum of Squares	df	Mean Square	F	Sig.
	Regression	1044.354	2	522.177	36.995	.000[a]
1	Residual	169.380	12	14.115		
	Total	1213.733	14			

a. Predictors: (Constant), me, mf

b. Dependent Variable: ap

Coefficients[a]

Model		Unstandardized Coefficients		Standardized Coefficients	t	Sig.	Collinearity Statistics	
		B	Std. Error	Beta			Tolerance	VIF
1	(Constant)	-16.151	7.965		-2.028	.065		
	mf	1.063	.922	.289	1.153	.271	.185	5.418
	me	2.089	.797	.658	2.621	.022	.185	5.418

a. Dependent Variable: ap

Collinearity Diagnostics[a]

Model	Dimension	Eigenvalue	Condition Index	Variance Proportions		
				(Constant)	mf	me
1	1	2.983	1.000	.00	.00	.00
	2	.015	14.233	.62	.01	.12
	3	.002	39.633	.37	.99	.88

a. Dependent Variable: ap

As it can be seen from the 4th table. The values of VIF for all two variables are more than 5. So, we have evidence of Multi-co linearity effect. However, one of these two variables is more important than other one. In 4th table, we can see that the p-value of ME is 0.022 which is less than $\alpha = 0.05$. On the other hand p-value of MF is 0.271 which is more than 0.05. So, according to the value of p-value ME is much important than MF. For confirming this issue, same process is done. However, the method is adjusted in STEP WISE. So, we hire the previous process again. However, the method is put in STEP WISE. (Figure 63)

Analyze ⇨ regression ⇨ linear ⇨ ………………

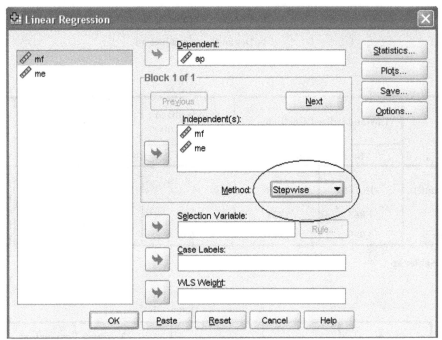

Figure 63

After pressing the ok button the output is caught.

Variables Entered/Removed[a]

Model	Variables Entered	Variables Removed	Method
1	me	.	Stepwise (Criteria: Probability-of-F-to-enter <= .050, Probability-of-F-to-remove >= .100).

a. Dependent Variable: ap

Model Summary

Model	R	R Square	Adjusted R Square	Std. Error of the Estimate
1	.919[a]	.845	.833	3.80420

a. Predictors: (Constant), me

ANOVA[b]

Model		Sum of Squares	df	Mean Square	F	Sig.
1	Regression	1025.598	1	1025.598	70.868	.000[a]
	Residual	188.136	13	14.472		
	Total	1213.733	14			

a. Predictors: (Constant), me

b. Dependent Variable: ap

Coefficients[a]

Model		Unstandardized Coefficients		Standardized Coefficients	t	Sig.	Collinearity Statistics	
		B	Std. Error	Beta			Tolerance	VIF
1	(Constant)	-9.899	5.907		-1.676	.118		
	me	2.919	.347	.919	8.418	.000	1.000	1.000

a. Dependent Variable: ap

Excluded Variables[b]

Model		Beta In	t	Sig.	Partial Correlation	Collinearity Statistics		
						Tolerance	VIF	Minimum Tolerance
1	mf	.289[a]	1.153	.271	.316	.185	5.418	.185

a. Predictors in the Model: (Constant), me

b. Dependent Variable: ap

Collinearity Diagnostics[a]

Model	Dimension	Eigenvalue	Condition Index	Variance Proportions	
				(Constant)	me
1	1	1.986	1.000	.01	.01
	2	.014	11.943	.99	.99

a. Dependent Variable: ap

As it is revealed from the 5th table, MF is located in excluded variables table and MF is not considered an important variable.

Report:

We tested the frame work using multiple regression .Based on the results, regression model is significant (F-value=70.868,P-value=0.000)
With an R square value of 0.845.This implies that 84.5%of the variance in the dependent variable (AP) can be explained by independent variable (ME).Out of the two independent variable, only ME is significant. The correlation table and collinearity statistics (VIF=5.418) indicate there is a multi-collinearity effect. Therefore, we used step-wise regression to get the results.
Review of the steps:
1. Run bi-variate correlation
-if independent variables are strongly correlated, there is a possibility of multi-collinearity effect.
2. Run the complete regression model with collinearity diagnostics and extra method.
If VIF> 5, there is evidence of multi collinearity, go to next step.
3. Run step-wise regression and interpret results.

Chapter 14: Mediating and Moderating Effects

Mediation Effect

Different kinds of mediation effect:
a. partial mediating: independent variable has a strong relationship with dependent variable and mediation effect is also strong
b. pure mediating: only mediation effect is strong.
To test for mediation effect, **Sobels test** is hired.

Example 1-14 :(Mediation)
Refer to example 3 from chapter 13.

Steps involved in testing mediation effect.

First, related regressions are described.
Regression 1:
MF is independent variable
ME is dependent variable
Regression 2:
MF and ME are independent variables
AP is dependent variable
Regression 3:
MF is independent variable
AP is dependent variable
Then ,
- Perform Sobels test with t_{MF-ME} and t_{ME-AP}

(t_{MF-ME} comes from regression 1)(t_{ME-AP} comes from regression 2)

Each regression is entered in linear regression window (analyze ⇨ regression ⇨ linear) and after clicking on ok button the result is got for each regression.

Regression one:

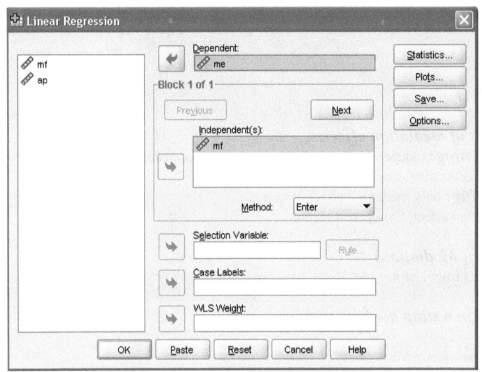

Figure 64

Variables Entered/Removed[b]

Mo del	Variables Entered	Variables Removed	Meth od
1	mf[a]	.	Enter

a. All requested variables entered.

b. Dependent Variable: me

Model Summary

Mod el	R	R Square	Adjusted R Square	Std. Error of the Estimate
1	.903[a]	.815	.801	1.30744

a. Predictors: (Constant), mf

ANOVA[b]

Model		Sum of Squares	df	Mean Square	F	Sig.
1	Regression	98.178	1	98.178	57.434	.000[a]
	Residual	22.222	13	1.709		
	Total	120.400	14			

a. Predictors: (Constant), mf

b. Dependent Variable: me

Coefficients[a]

Model		Unstandardized Coefficients		Standardized Coefficients	t	Sig.
		B	Std. Error	Beta		
1	(Constant)	-3.044	2.640		-1.153	.270
	mf	1.044	.138	.903	7.579	.000

a. Dependent Variable: me

Regression two:

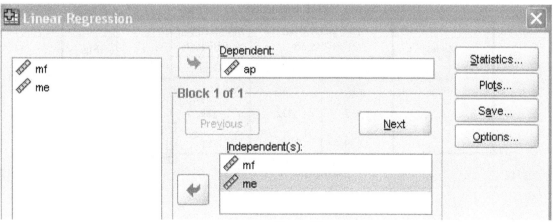

Figure 65

Variables Entered/Removed

Model	Variables Entered	Variables Removed	Method
1	me, mf[a]	.	Enter

a. All requested variables entered.

Model Summary

Model	R	R Square	Adjusted R Square	Std. Error of the Estimate
1	.928[a]	.860	.837	3.75699

a. Predictors: (Constant), me, mf

ANOVA[b]

Model		Sum of Squares	df	Mean Square	F	Sig.
1	Regression	1044.354	2	522.177	36.995	.000[a]
	Residual	169.380	12	14.115		
	Total	1213.733	14			

a. Predictors: (Constant), me, mf

b. Dependent Variable: ap

Coefficients[a]

Model		Unstandardized Coefficients		Standardized Coefficients	t	Sig.
		B	Std. Error	Beta		
1	(Constant)	-16.151	7.965		-2.028	.065
	mf	1.063	.922	.289	1.153	.271
	me	2.089	.797	.658	2.621	.022

a. Dependent Variable: ap

Regression three:

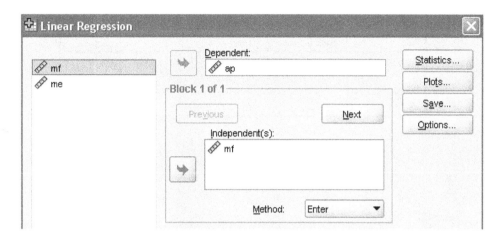

Figure 66

Variables Entered/Removed[b]

Mo del	Variables Entered	Variables Removed	Metho d
1	mf[a]	.	Enter

a. All requested variables entered.

b. Dependent Variable: ap

Model Summary

Mo del	R	R Square	Adjusted R Square	Std. Error of the Estimate
1	.883[a]	.781	.764	4.52647

a. Predictors: (Constant), mf

ANOVA[b]

Model		Sum of Squares	df	Mean Square	F	Sig.
1	Regression	947.378	1	947.378	46.239	.000[a]
	Residual	266.356	13	20.489		
	Total	1213.733	14			

a. Predictors: (Constant), mf

b. Dependent Variable: ap

Coefficients[a]

Model		Unstandardized Coefficients		Standardized Coefficients	t	Sig.
		B	Std. Error	Beta		
1	(Constant)	-22.511	9.141		-2.463	.029
	mf	3.244	.477	.883	6.800	.000

a. Dependent Variable: ap

Then, type Sobels test in a search engine in the internet or go to this address:

http://www.people.ku.edu/~preacher/sobel/sobel.htm

Enter the values (which are got from tables from regression one and two) in specific places as it is shown in picture and press the calculate button.

$$t_a = t_{MF-ME} = 7.579 \rightarrow \text{regression1}$$
$$t_b = t_{ME-AP} = 2.621 \rightarrow \text{regression2}$$

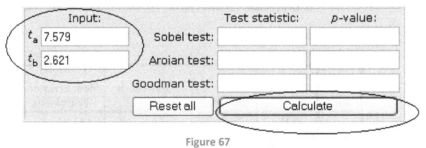

Figure 67

The following results are got:

Input:		Test statistic:	p-value:
t_a 7.579	Sobel test:	2.477	0.013
t_b 2.621	Aroian test:	2.45	0.013
	Goodman test:	2.49	0.012

Figure 68

Sobel test = 2.47706
P-value = 0.013246

Report:
H_1 : market focus has a positive relationship with market expansion
H_2 : market expansion has a positive relationship with acquisition performance
H_3 : market expansion mediates the relationship between market focus and acquisition performance.

To test the mediation effect of market expansion between market focus and acquisition performance, we performed Sobels test. Based on the results of sobels test (t=2.477, p-value=0.013), we conclude that market expansion mediates the relationship between market focus and acquisition performance.

Since market focus has a significant direct effect (t-value =6.80, p-value=0.000) on acquisition performance, market expansion has a partial mediating effect.

*NOTICE: The sobels test should be done only when the results from regressions show that the relationship between MF and ME as well as ME and AP is significant. Otherwise there is not mediating effect and no need to do sobels test.

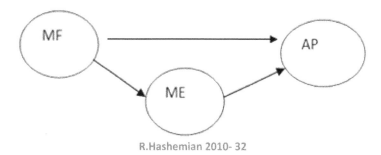

R.Hashemian 2010- 32

*NOTICE: The regression three in above example is for finding if the mediating effect is pure or partial. If the relationship between IV and DV is significant, mediating effect is partial. Otherwise, it is pure.

Sobel test in brief:

In **psychwiki.com** the importance and limitations of Sobel test has been stated as follows.
The Sobel test determines the significance of the indirect effect of the mediator by testing the hypothesis of no difference between the total effect (path c) and the direct effect (path c'). The indirect effect of the mediator is the product of path ab which is equivalent to (c - c'). (See Illustration 1)

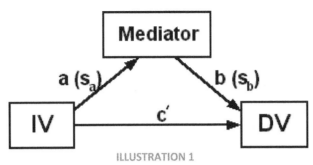

ILLUSTRATION 1

The Sobel test is superior to the Baron & Kenny(See the chapter one, Mediating variable) method in terms of all the limitations of the B&K method (e.g., power, Type I error, suppression effects, addressing the significance of the indirect effect)

Limitations of Sobel test:

The assumption for conducting the Sobel test (like most tests in psychology) is that the sampling distribution is normal. Hundreds of articles in statistical journals have shown that assumptions of normality are usually violated, especially in small samples, leading to reduced ability to detect true relationships amongst variables (see (Wilcox, 1998), (Wilcox, 2003), and (Wilcox, 2005) for more information).

Example 2-14 :(Moderating Effect)

Mesquita and Brush (2008) , in their article " untangling safeguard and production coordination effects in long trerm buyer – supplier relationship " published in academy of management journal have studied the relationship between inter -firm governance mechanisms and production efficiencies of firms. While analyzing this relationship, they have studied the effect of complexity of jobs between the two variables, governance mechanism and production efficiency (governance mechanism is the independent variable and the production efficiency is the dependent variable).Mesquita and Brush (2008:789) have explained the role of complexity as follows: "The degree of complexity can vary substantially from low to very high …. As complexity increase, the formal and informal governance mechanisms help improve production efficiencies. Thus, the effect of formal and informal mechanisms on production efficiencies is contingent upon level of complexity".

Suppose the summated scores on these three variables are as follows:

Trial	1	2	3	4	5	6	7	8	9	10	11	12	13	14	15
GM	35	30	37	43	30	32	33	37	38	40	41	42	36	45	44
PE	77	60	93	111	55	51	51	69	71	83	85	80	75	104	97
CY	27	29	35	38	30	28	30	30	28	34	40	39	31	30	40

GM-Governance mechanism, PE-Production efficiency, CY- Complexity

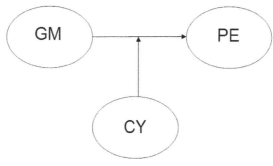

R.Hashemian 2010- 33

H_1 : GM has a positive relationship with PE.

H_2 : CY moderates the relationship between GM and PE.As CY increases formal and informal mechanism help improve PE.

For testing the hypotheses, we have to add another variable which describes the relationship between independent and moderating variables.

So, after entering the data following process is hired.

Transform ⇨ Compute variable

In target variable's part, GMCY is entered as name of new variable. Then, arrow key is used for moving the GM and CY to right side (GM*CY).

	GM	PE	CY
1	35.00	77.00	27.00
2	30.00	60.00	29.00
3	37.00	93.00	35.00
4	43.00	111.00	38.00
5	30.00	55.00	30.00
6	32.00	51.00	28.00
7	33.00	51.00	30.00
8	37.00	69.00	30.00
9	38.00	71.00	28.00
10	40.00	83.00	34.00
11	41.00	85.00	40.00
12	42.00	80.00	39.00
13	36.00	75.00	31.00
14	45.00	104.00	30.00
15	44.00	97.00	40.00

Figure 69

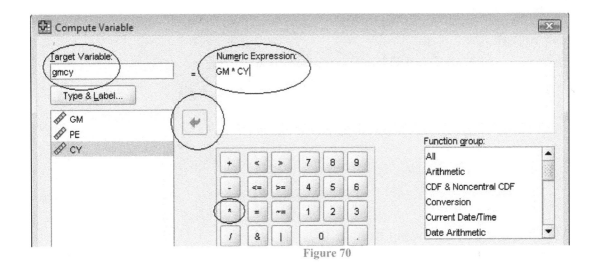

Figure 70

Next, we follow the process below.

Analyze ⇨ Regression ⇨ linear

While PE is entered as dependent, GMCY and GM are considered as independent ones.

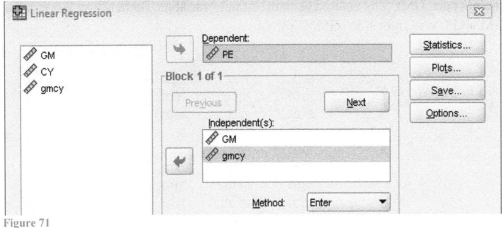

Figure 71

Finally press the ok and get the output.

Variables Entered/Removed

Mod el	Variables Entered	Variables Removed	Method
1	gmcy, GM[a]	.	Enter

a. All requested variables entered.

Model Summary

Model	R	R Square	Adjusted R Square	Std. Error of the Estimate
1	.874[a]	.764	.725	9.79046

a. Predictors: (Constant), gmcy, GM

ANOVA[b]

Model		Sum of Squares	df	Mean Square	F	Sig.
1	Regression	3725.495	2	1862.747	19.433	.000[a]
	Residual	1150.238	12	95.853		
	Total	4875.733	14			

a. Predictors: (Constant), gmcy, GM
b. Dependent Variable: PE

Coefficients[a]

Model		Unstandardized Coefficients		Standardized Coefficients	t	Sig.
		B	Std. Error	Beta		
1	(Constant)	-43.101	25.648		-1.680	.119
	GM	3.074	1.158	.812	2.655	.021
	gmcy	.004	.018	.070	.228	.823

a. Dependent Variable: PE

Report:

We tested the moderation effect of CY using multiple regression. Based on the results (t-value=0.228, p-value=0.823), CY does not moderate the relationship between GM and PE. *NOTICE: $0.823 > \alpha = 0.05 \Rightarrow$ we can not reject null hypothesis.

Chapter 15: Hierarchical regression

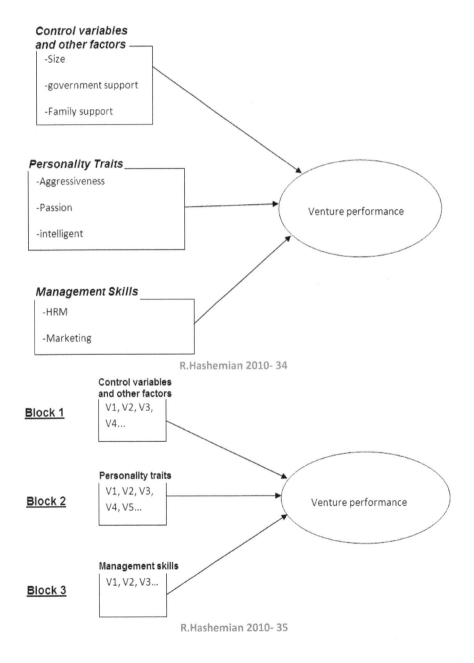

R.Hashemian 2010- 34

R.Hashemian 2010- 35

What is Hierarchical Regression?

As it can be seen from above illustration, venture performance is affected by different cases and per case has some other subs.

When we are involved with control variables as well as for illustrating the effect of variables as a group, hierarchical regression is hired. For example, for identifying the overall effect of personality traits and management skills in venture performance.

The control variables always are considered as the first group of variables.

Regarding the example above:

First group variables ➔ Control variables

Second group variables ➔ personality traits

Third group variables ➔ Management skills

MODEL 1	MODEL 2	MODEL 3
Control variable Vs Venture performance R^2	Control variable + Personality traits Vs Venture performance R^2 ΔR^2	Control variable + Personality traits + Management skills Vs Venture performance R^2 ΔR^2

We do the regression for all three models in table above.

Before giving an example the understanding of some terms which is appeared in output tables during the process is a necessity. These terms are as below.

Notice that the contents below were resourced from **UCLA academic technology services**.[1]

"Model - SPSS allows you to specify multiple models in a single **regression** command. This tells you the number of the model being reported.

---

[1]www.ats.ucla.edu/stat/spss/output/reg_spss.htm

Variables Entered - SPSS allows you to enter variables into a regression in blocks, and it allows stepwise regression. Hence, you need to know which variables were entered into the current regression. If you did not block your independent variables or use stepwise regression, this column should list all of the independent variables that you specified.

Variables Removed - This column listed the variables that were removed from the current regression. Usually, this column will be empty unless you did a stepwise regression.

Method - This column tells you the method that SPSS used to run the regression. "Enter" means that each independent variable was entered in usual fashion. If you did a stepwise regression, the entry in this column would tell you that.

R - R is the square root of R-Squared and is the correlation between the observed and predicted values of dependent variable.

R-Square - This is the proportion of variance in the dependent variable which can be explained by the independent variables. This is an overall measure of the strength of association and does not reflect the extent to which any particular independent variable is associated with the dependent variable.

Adjusted R-square - This is an adjustment of the R-squared that penalizes the addition of extraneous predictors to the model. Adjusted R-squared is computed using this formula : **1 - ((1 - Rsq) ((N - 1) / (N - k - 1))** where k is the number of predictors.

Std. Error of the Estimate - This is also referred to as the root mean squared error. It is the standard deviation of the error term and the square root of the Mean Square for the Residuals in the ANOVA table.

Regression, Residual, Total - Looking at the breakdown of variance in the outcome variable, these are the categories we will examine: Regression, Residual, and Total. The Total variance is partitioned into the variance which can be explained by the independent variables (Model) and the variance which is not explained by the independent variables (Error).

Sum of Squares - These are the Sum of Squares associated with the three sources of variance, Total, Model and Residual. The Total variance is partitioned into the variance which can be explained by the independent variables (Regression) and the variance which is not explained by the independent variables (Residual).

df - These are the degrees of freedom associated with the sources of variance. The total variance has N-1 degrees of freedom. The Regression degree of freedom corresponds to the number of coefficients estimated minus 1. The Error degree of freedom is the DF total minus the DF model.

Mean Square - These are the Mean Squares, the Sum of Squares divided by their respective DF.

F and **Sig.** - This is the F-statistic the p-value associated with it. The F-statistic is the Mean Square (Regression) divided by the Mean Square (Residual). The p-value is compared to some alpha level in testing the null hypothesis that all of the model coefficients are 0."

Example1-15:

Refer to example 1 from chapter 12:

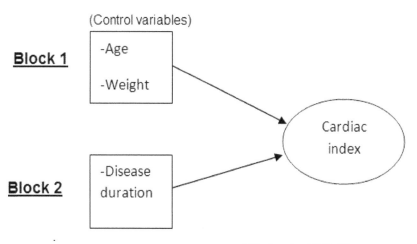

R.Hashemian 2010- 36

After entering the data, the process below is followed.
Analyze ⇨ Regression ⇨ Linear
First, the cardiac index is moved to dependent part as well as age and weight to independent part. Then, click on next button and shift the duration to independent part.(Refer to definition of control variable in previous chapters)
Click on statistics button and tick the R squared change.
Finally, press the continue, ok and get the output.

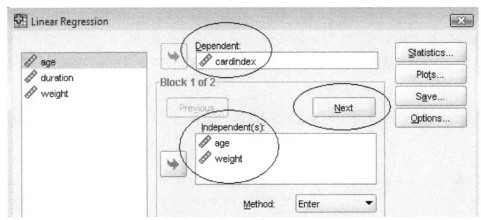

Figure 72

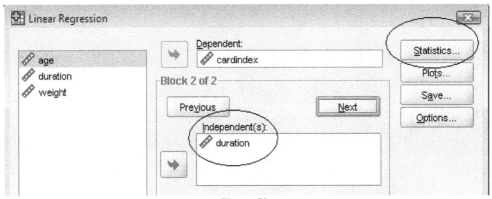

Figure 73

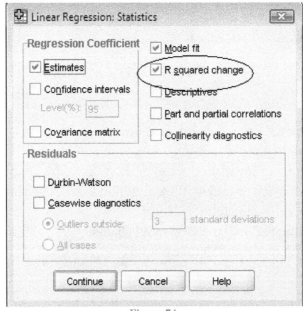

Figure 74

Variables Entered/Removed[b]

Model	Variables Entered	Variables Removed	Method
1	weight, age[a]	.	Enter
2	duration[a]	.	Enter

a. All requested variables entered.

b. Dependent Variable: cardindex

Model Summary

Model	R	R Square	Adjusted R Square	Std. Error of the Estimate	Change Statistics				
					R Square Change	F Change	df1	df2	Sig. F Change
1	.901[a]	.812	.759	.21153	.812	15.149	2	7	.003
2	.907[b]	.822	.733	.22257	.010	.323	1	6	.590

a. Predictors: (Constant), weight, age

b. Predictors: (Constant), weight, age, duration

ANOVA[c]

	Model	Sum of Squares	df	Mean Square	F	Sig.
1	Regression	1.356	2	.678	15.149	.003[a]
	Residual	.313	7	.045		
	Total	1.669	9			
2	Regression	1.372	3	.457	9.230	.011[b]
	Residual	.297	6	.050		
	Total	1.669	9			

a. Predictors: (Constant), weight, age

b. Predictors: (Constant), weight, age, duration

c. Dependent Variable: cardindex

Coefficients[a]

Model		Unstandardized Coefficients		Standardized Coefficients	t	Sig.
		B	Std. Error	Beta		
1	(Constant)	3.739	.602		6.213	.000
	age	-.041	.008	-.865	-5.283	.001
	weight	.008	.005	.263	1.608	.152
2	(Constant)	3.831	.653		5.862	.001
	age	-.042	.008	-.888	-5.019	.002
	weight	.007	.006	.233	1.290	.244
	duration	.019	.033	.105	.568	.590

a. Dependent Variable: cardindex

Excluded Variables[b]

Model		Beta In	t	Sig.	Partial Correlation	Collinearity Statistics Tolerance
1	duration	.105[a]	.568	.590	.226	.867

a. Predictors in the Model: (Constant), weight, age

b. Dependent Variable: cardindex

Model1 ➔ R^2 = 0.812, F change = 15.149, p-value (Sig. F Change) = 0.003 < α = 0.05
Model 2 ➔ R^2 = 0.822, F change = 0.323, p-value (Sig. F Change) = 0.590 > α = 0.05
This implies that the second block of variables (Disease duration) has not added significantly to R^2 (ΔR^2 = 0.010, F change = 0.323, p-value (Sig. F Change) = 0.590).So, results reveal that block 1 has significant effect on dependent variable.

Chapter 16: Logistic Regression

Different Types of Logistic Regression:
a. Binary logistic regression
b. Multinomial logistic regression

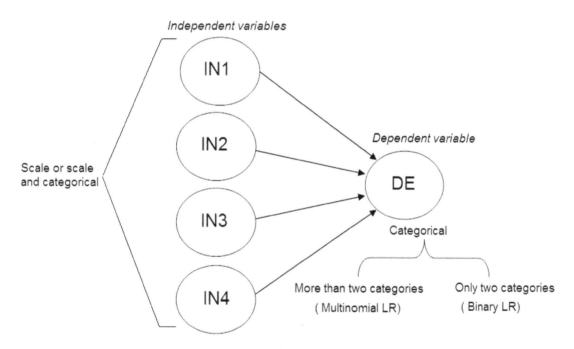

R.Hashemian 2010- 37

As it is revealed from illustration above, if our independent variables were scale or a combination of scale and categorical as well as our dependent variable was categorical, logistic regression is hired. Furthermore, if our dependent variable was only 2 categories, Binary logistic regression is used. However, for more than two categories Multinomial logistic regression is hired.

*NOTICE:

*If the nature of DE was ordinal or nominal, the multiple regression cannot be used and logistic regression is hired.

*In more complicated issues, MDA (Multiple Discriminant Analysis) is used instead of logistic regression.

-If the values that dependent variable can get is 0 or 1, we would have two categories.
For instance:
Are people interested to purchase X?   Yes (y=0), No (y=1)

Multiple regression model ➜ $y = a + b1x1 + b2 x2 + ... + e$

Logistic regression model ➜ $P_r(y=1/x) = \dfrac{e^{B0+B1X1+B2X2+\cdots}}{1+e^{B0+B1X1+B2X2+\cdots}}$

P_r = probability, X = Independent variable

Following the example above, P_r shows the probability of purchasing X regarding the Each of independent variables(X1, X2...).

If probability ≥ 0.5 ➜ Y=1
If probability ≤ 0.5 ➜ Y=0

EXAMPLE1-16:

KL diabetic center wants (1) to determine the relationship between relative weight (RW) , fasting plasma glucose (FPG) , test plasma glucose (TPG) , plasma insulin during test (PIDT) , steady state plasma glucose (SSPG) with the type of diabetes (TY) and (2) develop a regression model to predict the type of diabetes. There are two types of diabetes: Overt diabetic and chemically diabetic. The data collected on 25 patients is as follows (RW, FPG, TPG, PIDT, SSPG, and TY):

RW	FPG	TPG	PIDT	SSPG	TY
0.95	96.00	356.00	112.00	73.00	1.00
1.03	88.00	291.00	157.00	122.00	1.00
0.87	87.00	360.00	292.00	128.00	1.00
0.87	94.00	313.00	200.00	233.00	1.00
1.17	93.00	306.00	220.00	132.00	1.00
0.83	86.00	319.00	144.00	138.00	1.00
0.82	86.00	349.00	109.00	83.00	1.00
0.86	96.00	332.00	151.00	109.00	2.00
1.01	86.00	323.00	158.00	96.00	1.00
0.88	89.00	323.00	73.00	52.00	1.00
0.75	83.00	351.00	81.00	42.00	1.00
0.99	98.00	478.00	151.00	122.00	2.00
1.12	100.00	398.00	122.00	176.00	1.00
1.09	110.00	426.00	117.00	118.00	1.00
1.02	88.00	439.00	208.00	244.00	2.00
1.19	100.00	429.00	201.00	194.00	2.00
1.06	80.00	333.00	131.00	136.00	1.00
1.20	89.00	472.00	162.00	257.00	2.00
1.05	91.00	436.00	148.00	167.00	2.00
1.10	90.00	413.00	344.00	270.00	2.00
1.03	100.00	385.00	192.00	180.00	1.00
1.08	94.00	426.00	213.00	177.00	2.00
1.19	85.00	425.00	143.00	204.00	2.00
0.95	111.00	558.00	748.00	122.00	2.00
1.06	107.00	503.00	320.00	253.00	1.00

First, the data is entered. (Figure 75)

	RW	FPG	TPG	PIDT	SSPG	TY
1	0.95	96.00	356.00	112.00	73.00	1.00
2	1.03	88.00	291.00	157.00	122.00	1.00
3	0.87	87.00	360.00	292.00	128.00	1.00
4	0.87	94.00	313.00	200.00	233.00	1.00
21	1.03	100.00	385.00	192.00	180.00	1.00
22	1.08	94.00	426.00	213.00	177.00	2.00
23	1.19	85.00	425.00	143.00	204.00	2.00
24	0.95	111.00	558.00	748.00	122.00	2.00
25	1.06	107.00	503.00	320.00	253.00	1.00

Figure 75

Then, following process is hired.

Analyze ⇨ regression ⇨ Binary logistic (we have only two dependent categories)

In logistic regression window TY is moved to dependent part and the rest of variables are shifted to covariate part.

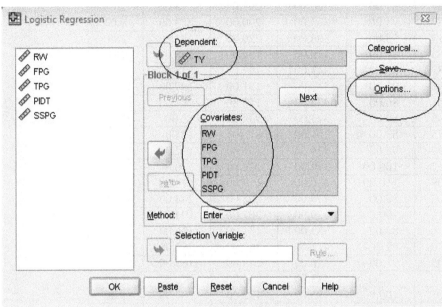

Figure 76

Next, click on options button and select Hosmer – Lemesshow goodness-of-fit.

77 Figure

Finally, click on continue and ok and get the output.

Logistic Regression

Case Processing Summary

Unweighted Cases[a]		N	Percent
Selected Cases	Included in Analysis	25	100.0
	Missing Cases	0	.0
	Total	25	100.0
Unselected Cases		0	.0
Total		25	100.0

a. If weight is in effect, see classification table for the total number of cases.

Dependent Variable Encoding

Original Value	Internal Value
1.00	0
2.00	1

Block 0: Beginning Block

Classification Table[a,b]

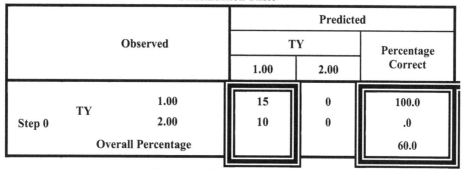

	Observed		Predicted		
			TY		Percentage Correct
			1.00	2.00	
Step 0	TY	1.00	15	0	100.0
		2.00	10	0	.0
	Overall Percentage				60.0

a. Constant is included in the model.

b. The cut value is .500

Variables in the Equation

		B	S.E.	Wald	df	Sig.	Exp(B)
Step 0	Constant	-.405	.408	.986	1	.321	.667

Variables not in the Equation

			Score	df	Sig.
Step 0	Variables	RW	3.396	1	.065
		FPG	.324	1	.569
		TPG	9.471	1	.002
		PIDT	2.539	1	.111
		SSPG	4.661	1	.031
	Overall Statistics		12.469	5	.029

Block 1: Method = Enter

Omnibus Tests of Model Coefficients

		Chi-square	df	Sig.
Step 1	Step	14.713	5	.012
	Block	14.713	5	.012
	Model	14.713	5	.012

Model Summary

Step	-2 Log likelihood	Cox & Snell R Square	Nagelkerke R Square
1	18.938[a]	.445	.601

a. Estimation terminated at iteration number 6 because parameter estimates changed by less than .001.

Hosmer and Lemeshow Test

Step	Chi-square	df	Sig.
1	15.480	6	.017

Contingency Table for Hosmer and Lemeshow Test

		TY = 1.00		TY = 2.00		Total
		Observed	Expected	Observed	Expected	
Step 1	1	2	2.921	1	.079	3
	2	3	2.836	0	.164	3
	3	3	2.664	0	.336	3
	4	3	2.563	0	.437	3
	5	3	2.121	0	.879	3
	6	0	.974	3	2.026	3
	7	1	.611	2	2.389	3
	8	0	.310	4	3.690	4

Classification Table[a]

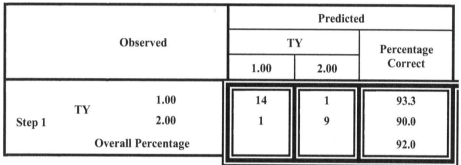

	Observed		Predicted		
			TY		Percentage Correct
			1.00	2.00	
Step 1	TY	1.00	14	1	93.3
		2.00	1	9	90.0
	Overall Percentage				92.0

a. The cut value is .500

Variables in the Equation

		B	S.E.	Wald	df	Sig.	Exp(B)
Step 1[a]	RW	4.507	7.321	.379	1	.538	90.676
	FPG	-.156	.102	2.318	1	.128	.856
	TPG	.034	.016	4.266	1	.039	1.035
	PIDT	.001	.007	.033	1	.857	1.001
	SSPG	.000	.015	.001	1	.976	1.000
	Constant	- 4.112	7.668	.288	1	.592	.016

a. Variable(s) entered on step 1: RW, FPG, TPG, PIDT, SSPG.

Logistic regression outputs:
a. Overall fit statistics
b. Significant of individual variables statistics

Overall fit statistics:

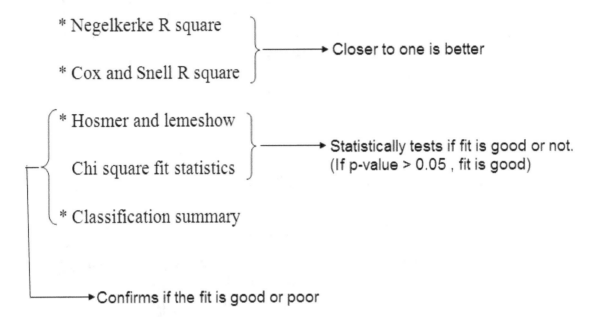

*NOTICE:

If p-value < 0.05 ➜ Fit is not good and the significant level for α =0.01 should be calculated as well.

Once the model is obtained for given values of X (RW, FPG, TPG, PIDT, SSPG), the model predicts the value of TY as 1 or 2 from the expression $P_r(y=1/x) = \frac{e^{B0+B1X1+B2X2+\cdots}}{1+e^{B0+B1X1+B2X2+\cdots}}$ .The mentioned expression calculates the probability. If probability $\geq$ 0.5, TY is predicted as 2 and if probability $<$ 0.5, TY is predicted as 1.So, it is done as process below.

Regarding the gotten results from table of variables, the elements of equation are replaced with values from mentioned table and logistic regression equation comes as follows.

$$P_r(y=1/x) = \frac{e^{-4.112+(4.507*RW)-(0.156*FPG)+(0.034*TPG)+(0.001*PIDT)+(0.000*SSPG)}}{1+e^{-4.112+(4.507*RW)-(0.156*FPG)+(0.034*TPG)+(0.001*PIDT)+(0.000*SSPG)}}$$

Then, replace the related elements of the equation with the values in first row are given in the data table.

RW	FPG	TPG	PIDT	SSPG
0.95	96.00	356.00	112.00	73.00

$$P_r(y=1/x) = \frac{e^{-4.112+(4.507*0.95)-(0.156*96)+(0.034*356)+(0.001*112)+(0.000*73)}}{1+e^{e^{-4.112+(4.507*0.95)-(0.156*96)+(0.034*356)+(0.001*112)+(0.000*73)}}}$$

Next, the equation is calculated. If probability(P_r) $\geq$ 0.5, TY is predicted as 2 and if probability < 0.5, TY is predicted as 1.

As it can be revealed from classification table in Block 1, we had 15 predicts for TY=1 and 14 predicts out of 15 predicts were predicted correctly and one was predicted wrongly.

Regarding TY=2, there were 10 predicts. One predict out of 10 predicts was wrong.

In Block 0 the classification table is shown .There are 15 predictions for TY=1 and 10 predictions for TY=2.

15/25*100 = 60%, 10/25*100 = 40%

As it is seen the highest value is 60%. The overall percentage correct which is 60 % is illustrated in last row of table. 60 % is called threshold value. If in classification table in Block one the overall percentage correct is more than threshold value, model is good.

Review:

In classification table from Block 1, there are 15 observations which only 14 of them were predicted correctly and in second column we have 10 observations which 9 were predicated correctly. In general, 92 % predicted correctly. Furthermore, 60% from Block0 is called threshold value. 92% > 60% ➔ the model is fit.

Threshold value = 60%

Nagel karke R square = 0.601

Cox & sne4ll R square = 0.445

Hosmer & lemeshow chi-square = 15.480

P-value = 0.017

 If the overall correct percentage was more than threshold value, we would test the significance of variables. So, we refer to table of variables in the equation .As it is revealed from mentioned table only TPG is important. Since, the p – value of TPG is 0.039.It can be seen that only the p-value of TPG is less than 0.05 and the rest are more than 0.05.

Of all the independent variables only TPG has a significant impact on type of diabetes (Wald – statistics = 4.266, p-value = 0.039)

Example 2-16:

A researcher wants to study if the perception of customers about a product is positive or negative. The researcher collects responses from 100 customers on the following seven variables: Competitive pricing, price flexibility, product quality , technical support , advertising , delivery speed , and perception of customers . The researcher ran a logistic regression model and the output are as follows:

Cox and Snell R-square = 0.505; Nagelkarke R – square = 0.677; Hosmer and Lemeshow Chi-square = 5.326 and Significant probability = 0.722

Variable	B	Wald	Sig.prob
Comp.pricing	1.079	9.115	0.003
Price flex	1.844	14.614	0.004

Observed	Predicted Perception		Age%
	+	-	
Perception +	34	5	34
Overall -	8	53	53

34/39 * 100 = 87.17
53/61 *100 = 86.88
(53+34)/100 = 87%. In this example 87% is predicted correctly.

Example 3-16:

Study given in the following table with y=1 if the project was successfully completed in the allocated time and y= 0 if the project was not successfully completed.

Months of Experience	Project Success	Months of Experience	Project Success
2	0	15	1
4	0	16	1
5	0	17	0
6	0	19	1
7	0	20	1
8	1	22	0
8	1	23	1
9	0	24	1
10	0	27	1
10	0	30	0
11	1	31	1
12	1	32	1
13	0		

a. Use the computer output given here to determine whether experience is associated with the probability of completing the task.

b. Compute the probability of successfully completing the task for an engineer having 24 months of experience. Place 95%confidence interval on your estimation.

First variables are described and data is entered.
Two variables are entered. **Result (nominal)** and **Experience (scale)**. For result, two values are described, **Fail** and **Success**.

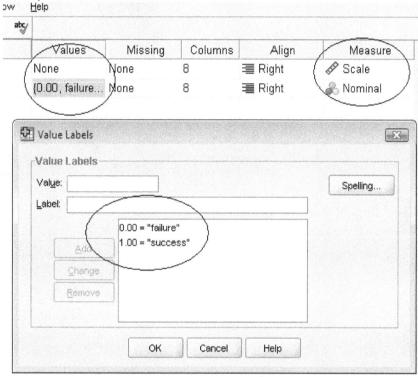

Figure 78

	exp	result
1	2.00	0.00
2	4.00	0.00
3	5.00	0.00
4	6.00	0.00
5	7.00	0.00
22	27.00	1.00
23	30.00	0.00
24	31.00	1.00
25	32.00	1.00

Figure79

IND. Variable ➔ EXP

DEP. Variable ➔ RESULT ➔ Nominal ➔ 0(failure) and 1(success)

Then, following process is hired.

Analyze ⇨ regression ⇨ Binary logistic (we have only two dependent categories)

In logistic regression window RESULT is moved to dependent part and EXP is shifted to covariate part.

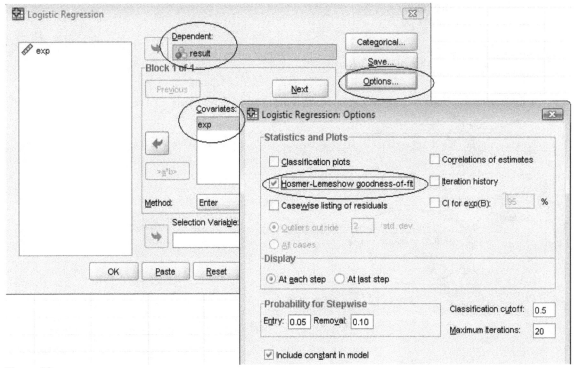

Figure 80

Follow the same process with previous question and press the continue and ok button. Finally, get the output.

Logistic Regression

Case Processing Summary

Unweighted Cases[a]		N	Percent
Selected Cases	Included in Analysis	25	100.0
	Missing Cases	0	.0
	Total	25	100.0
Unselected Cases		0	.0
Total		25	100.0

a. If weight is in effect, see classification table for the total number of cases.

Dependent Variable Encoding

Original Value	Internal Value
failure	0
success	1

Block 0: Beginning Block

Classification Table[a,b]

			Predicted		
			result		Percentage Correct
Observed			failure	success	
Step 0	result	failure	0	12	.0
		success	0	13	100.0
	Overall Percentage				52.0

a. Constant is included in the model.

b. The cut value is .500

Variables in the Equation

		B	S.E.	Wald	df	Sig.	Exp(B)
Step 0	Constant	.080	.400	.040	1	.842	1.083

Variables not in the Equation

			Score	df	Sig.
Step 0	Variables	exp	4.833	1	.028
	Overall Statistics		4.833	1	.028

Block 1: Method = Enter

Omnibus Tests of Model Coefficients

		Chi-square	df	Sig.
Step 1	Step	5.244	1	.022
	Block	5.244	1	.022
	Model	5.244	1	.022

Model Summary

Step	-2 Log likelihood	Cox & Snell R Square	Nagelkerke R Square
1	29.374[a]	.189	.252

a. Estimation terminated at iteration number 4 because parameter estimates changed by less than .001.

Hosmer and Lemeshow Test

Step	Chi-square	df	Sig.
1	6.329	6	.387

Contingency Table for Hosmer and Lemeshow Test

		result = failure		result = success		Total
		Observed	Expected	Observed	Expected	
Step 1	1	3	2.327	0	.673	3
	2	2	2.774	2	1.226	4
	3	3	1.888	0	1.112	3
	4	1	1.687	2	1.313	3
	5	1	1.332	2	1.668	3
	6	1	.970	2	2.030	3
	7	0	.669	3	2.331	3
	8	1	.354	2	2.646	3

Classification Table[a]

			Predicted		
	Observed		result		Percentage Correct
			failure	success	
Step 1	result	failure	9	3	75.0
		success	4	9	69.2
	Overall Percentage				72.0

a. The cut value is .500

Variables in the Equation

		B	S.E.	Wald	df	Sig.	Exp(B)
Step 1[a]	exp	.119	.059	4.109	1	.043	1.127
	Constant	-1.684	.945	3.176	1	.075	.186

a. Variable(s) entered on step 1: exp.

$$\begin{cases} \text{Cox \& Snell R Square} = 0.189 \\ \text{Nagelkerke R Square} = 0.252 \end{cases}$$

$$\begin{cases} \textbf{Hosmer and Lemeshow Test} \\ \text{Chi-square} = 6.329, \text{df} = 6, \text{p-value} = 0.387 \ (0.387 > 0.05) \rightarrow \text{Model fit is good} \end{cases}$$

Classification summary:

Regarding the classification table from block 0 ➔ Threshold value = 52% (prediction capability of the model must be more than 52%)

Regarding the classification table from block 1 ➔ 72% > 52%

So, according to the classification tables' summary, fit of the model is good.

Next, we test the significance of variables. So, we refer to table of variables in the equation .As it is revealed from mentioned table p-value of experience is 0.043(less than 0.05) and wald = 4.109 .Thus, experience has a significant impact in project success.

Experience has a positive relationship with project success. This is because, the sign of coefficient (0.119) is positive. So, for each unit increase in the independent variable, the probability of the project's success (Result=1) is increased.

If the coefficient was negative, for each unit increase in the independent variable (experience), the probability of the project's failure (Result = 0) would be increased.

*NOTICE:

The analysis of the coefficients belong to independent variables in logistic regression is different from multiple regression ones. In logistic regression the amount of change in dependent variable cannot be predicted regarding the amount of coefficient of independent variable. And only the sign (+, -) of the coefficient in independent variables can show if 0 or 1 is allocated to the dependent variable.

Regarding the gotten results from table of variables, the elements of equation are replaced with values from mentioned table and logistic regression equation comes as follows

$$P_r(y=1/x) = \frac{e^{-1.684+(0.119*EXP)}}{1+e^{-1.684+(0.119*EXP)}}$$

Then, replace the related elements of the equation with the values in first row are given in the data table.

Months of Experience
2

$$P_r(y=1/x) = \frac{e^{-1.684+(0.119*2)}}{1+e^{-1.684+(0.119*2)}}$$

Next, the equation is calculated. If probability(P_r) $\geq$ 0.5, TY is predicted as 1 and if probability < 0.5, TY is predicted as 0.

Report:
In order to test the relationship between months of experience and result of project (Success =1, Failure = 0), we ran a logistic regression model. Based on the results we can observe the following:
-Prediction capability of the model is 72 %(threshold value is 52%)
-Hosmer and Lemeshow test indicates a chi-square value of 6.329 and p-value of 0.387.
-combining the above two results shows that model fit is good.
-There is a positive relationship between months of experience and result of the project. As months of experience are increased, probability of project success is increased.

Chapter 17: Reliability and Validity

What are Reliability and Validity?

- Questionnaire items that capture attitude / behavior / perception
- Reliability indicates how consistent the responses are
- Validity measures if the items under a construct are actually explaining / measuring that construct.

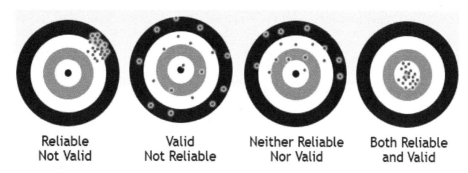

Figure 81

Reliability testing:

A lot of tests are exist for measuring the reliability. However, the best test is called Cronbach Alpha. Typical value for Cronbach Alpha must be greater than 0.70. (Nunnally 1976).

Example 1-17:

Data for this example can be downloaded from link below or contact the author.

http://fepb.mihanblog.com/

Let say we entered data as follows. (All data is not shown in figure and only related one is illustrated):

	OPEN001	OPEN002	OPEN003	OPEN004	OPEN005	OPEN006	OPEN007	PATCON008	PATCON009	PATCON0'
1	5.00	5.00	5.00	5.00	5.00	5.00	5.00	3.00	5.00	5.00
2	5.00	6.00	6.00	7.00	6.00	6.00	5.00	5.00	4.00	4.00
3	5.00	4.00	5.00	5.00	6.00	6.00	6.00	6.00	7.00	6.00
4	5.00	5.00	5.00	6.00	5.00	5.00	6.00	5.00	5.00	6.00
5	6.00	7.00	5.00	6.00	7.00	7.00	4.00	5.00	5.00	6.00
6	1.00	6.00	7.00	6.00	7.00	7.00	5.00	4.00	5.00	4.00
7	6.00	6.00	6.00	7.00	6.00	6.00	6.00	6.00	6.00	7.00
8	5.00	5.00	6.00	5.00	6.00	5.00	6.00	5.00	6.00	4.00
9	5.00	6.00	6.00	5.00	4.00	6.00	3.00	6.00	5.00	6.00
10	4.00	2.00	5.00	6.00	6.00	5.00	4.00	5.00	5.00	7.00
11	6.00	6.00	7.00	7.00	6.00	7.00	7.00	7.00	6.00	6.00
12	6.00	6.00	7.00	7.00	6.00	7.00	7.00	7.00	6.00	6.00
13	6.00	6.00	6.00	6.00	4.00	7.00	6.00	6.00	5.00	6.00
14	7.00	5.00	7.00	7.00	6.00	7.00	6.00	6.00	5.00	6.00
15	6.00	6.00	7.00	7.00	6.00	6.00	6.00	6.00	6.00	6.00

Figure82

For evaluating of the reliability the following process must be hired.

Analyze ⇨ Scale ⇨ Reliability Analysis

In this case we are going to test the reliability of the variables from OPEN001 up to

OPEN007.So; we transfer the mentioned variables to right side.

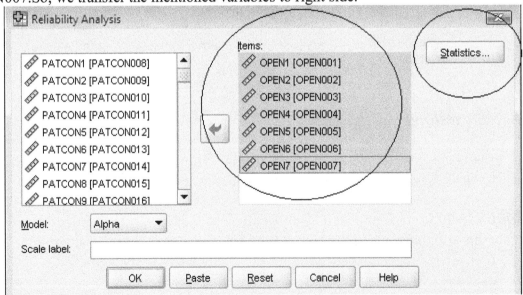

Figure 83

With clicking on statistics button, related part is opened .Select the Scale and Scale if item deleted and press continue

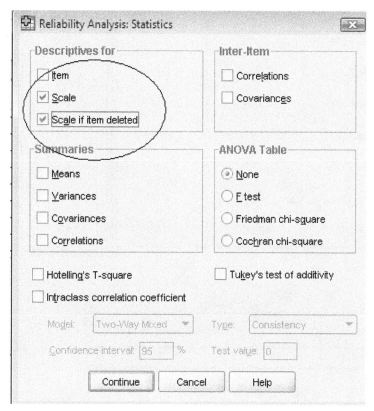

Figure84

Output is as follows.

Case Processing Summary

		N	%
Cases	Valid	150	98.7
	Excluded[a]	2	1.3
	Total	152	100.0

a. Listwise deletion based on all variables in the procedure.

Reliability Statistics

Cronbach's Alpha	N of Items
.860	7

Item-Total Statistics

	Scale Mean if Item Deleted	Scale Variance if Item Deleted	Corrected Item-Total Correlation	Cronbach's Alpha if Item Deleted
OPEN 1	36.5200	21.661	.529	.856
OPEN 2	36.5200	21.916	.539	.854
OPEN 3	36.0200	22.583	.616	.843
OPEN 4	36.1400	22.376	.671	.837
OPEN 5	36.2933	21.376	.630	.840
OPEN 6	36.4400	20.973	.710	.829
OPEN 7	36.5867	20.164	.740	.823

Scale Statistics

Mean	Variance	Std. Deviation	N of Items
42.4200	28.702	5.35739	7

The amount of Cronbach Alpha is 0.860 .So , reliability is good.Since , 0.860 > 0.70.

Example 2-17:

Data for this example can be downloaded from links below or contact the author.

http://fepb.mihanblog.com/

Let try the reliability test for another group of variables.For doing the test , same procedure is followed . However , in window of reliability analysis the reset button must be cilicked for cleaning the right side as well as preventing any kind of conflict with previous test.Then all the variables with name of PATCON are moved to right side and follow the mentioned procedure same as previous example.

7.00	6.00	7.00	7.00	6.00	7.00
5.00	5.00	6.00	7.00	6.00	7.00
7.00	7.00	6.00	5.00	6.00	7.00

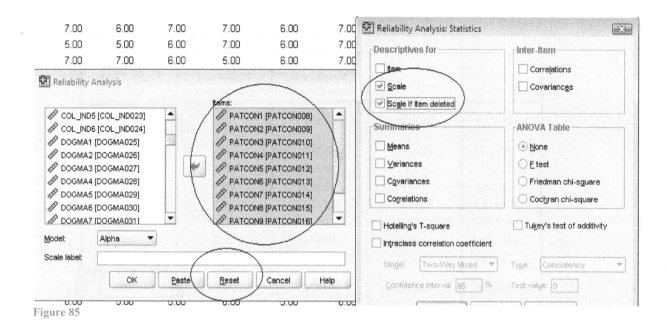

Figure 85

Output will be as follows.

Case Processing Summary

		N	%
Cases	Valid	148	97.4
	Excluded[a]	4	2.6
	Total	152	100.0

a. Listwise deletion based on all variables in the procedure.

Reliability Statistics

Cronbach's Alpha	N of Items
.780	11

Item-Total Statistics

	Scale Mean if Item Deleted	Scale Variance if Item Deleted	Corrected Item-Total Correlation	Cronbach's Alpha if Item Deleted
PATCON1	54.1419	61.891	.420	.764
PATCON2	54.6216	64.767	.331	.774
PATCON3	54.2162	60.946	.496	.756
PATCON4	54.1419	62.993	.359	.771
PATCON5	53.7162	64.654	.433	.765
PATCON6	54.2365	63.733	.438	.763
PATCON7	53.8919	60.655	.555	.750
PATCON8	54.3243	59.731	.447	.762
PATCON9	55.4595	59.270	.375	.775
PATCON10	55.0000	59.823	.508	.754
PATCON11	55.2365	60.944	.462	.760

Scale Statistics

Mean	Variance	Std. Deviation	N of Items
59.8986	73.126	8.55136	11

As it can be seen from table , value of Cronbach Alpha is equal to 0.780.It shows the reliability still is reasonable(0.780 > 0.7).However , reliability of previous example was more than this one.

*NOTICE:
With ticking the **scale** we can get the overall score as well as selecting the **Scale if item deleted** reveals the value of Cronbach Alpha if a particular item was deleted and it shows that which item should be deleted for improving the Cronbach Alpha. For instance, the amount of **Cronbach Alpha if Item Deleted** for PAPCON 1 is 0.764.It means that if PAPCON 1 was cleaned from the data, amount of Cronbach Alpha comes 0.764.With cleaning the PATCON 9; the possible highest amount of Cronbach Alpha (0.775) can be got. However, it is not advisable any time, unless the Cronbach Alpha is less than 0.7. When report is written, the reason of excluding the variable and the effect on the value of Cronbach Alpha should be stated.

Validity testing:

For measuring validity, SPSS cannot be used and Confirmatory factor analysis is hired.

*NOTICE:
In statistics, **confirmatory factor analysis (CFA)** is a special form of factor analysis. It is used to test whether measures of a construct are consistent with a researcher's understanding of the nature of that construct (or factor). In contrast to exploratory factor analysis, where all loadings are free to vary, CFA allows for the explicit constraint of certain loadings to be zero. CFA has built upon and replaced older methods of analyzing construct validity such as the MTMM Matrix as described in Campbell & Fiske (1959).[19].

Construct validity:

1. Content validity: When you read the items whether they show what they suppose to show or not. There is not any statistical test for evaluating the content validity and some tools like focus group or Delphi should be hired.

2. Convergent validity:

Convergent validity, is the degree to which an operation is similar to (converges on) other operations that it theoretically should also be similar to. For instance, to show the convergent validity of a test of mathematics skills, the scores on the test can be correlated with scores on other tests that are also designed to measure basic mathematics ability. High correlations between the test scores would be evidence of a convergent validity. Convergent validity shows that the assessment is related to what it should theoretically be related to. It is ideal that scales rate high in discriminant validity as well, which unlike convergent validity is designed to measure the extent to which a given scale differs from other scales designed to measure a different conceptual variable. Discriminant validity and convergent validity are the two good ways to measure construct validity. The validity of a measure ought to be gauged by comparing it to measures of the same concept developed through other methods.[20].

3. Nomological validity:

You take the construct and put it in frame work. When you put it in that framework, it makes sense or not. Nomological validity is a form of construct validity. It is the degree to which a construct behaves as it should within a system of related constructs called a nomological set.

4. Scale validity:

Reading the article about *Scale Development* from *Moore and Benbasat* is advised.

Chapter 18: Factor Analysis

2 G. Meixner 1998

What is Factor analysis?
- Identify underlying dimensions of a construct.
- A construct may be uni-dimensional or multi-dimensional.
- Factor analysis helps us to determine if the construct is uni or multi dimensional.

Different kinds of Factor Analysis:

a. Exploratory Factor Analysis (EFA)
b. Confirmatory factor Analysis (CFA)

Factor Analysis	
Exploratory Factor Analysis(EFA)	**Confirmatory factor Analysis(CFA)**
We don't know what the underlying dimensions are	We know what the underlying dimensions are and the items under each dimensions
We want to uncover the underlying dimensions	We want to confirm if the items reflect a dimensions

With SPSS , EFA can be done. However, CFA should be done by other software such as, AMOS.

Example 1-18:

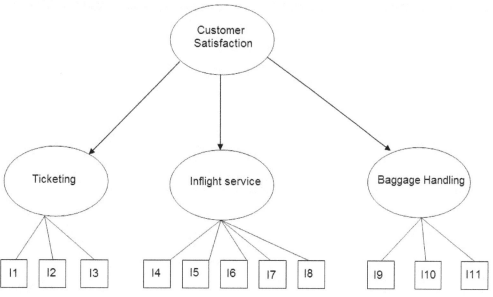

R.Hashemian 2010- 38

Customer satisfaction is affected by three dimensions. Each dimension has some items .Factor analysis groups these 11 items to one factor.

Example 2-18:

Data for this example can be downloaded from link below or contact the author.
http://fepb.mihanblog.com/
In this example name of our variable is CETSCALE (Consumer Ethnocentric Scale).
Before starting the test click on reset button to clean the materials of previous example.

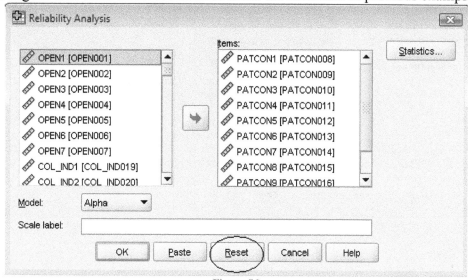

Figure 86

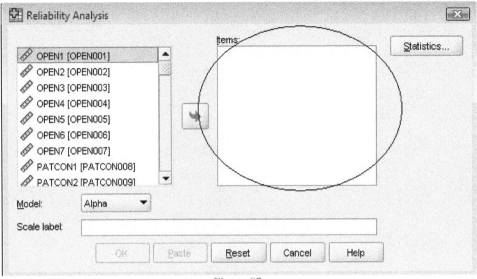

Figure 87

For doing factor analysis the following procedure is hired.

First, we do the reliability test. Reliability test is done as it was explained before.

Analysis ⇨ Scale ⇨ Reliability Analysis

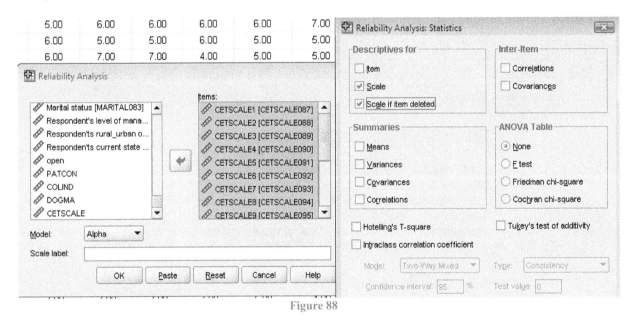

Figure 88

Output comes as follows.

Case Processing Summary

		N	%
Cases	Valid	144	94.7
	Excluded[a]	8	5.3
	Total	152	100.0

a. Listwise deletion based on all variables in the procedure.

Reliability Statistics

Cronbach's Alpha	N of Items
.910	17

Item-Total Statistics

	Scale Mean if Item Deleted	Scale Variance if Item Deleted	Corrected Item-Total Correlation	Cronbach's Alpha if Item Deleted
CETSCALE1	76.8750	390.670	.569	.906
CETSCALE2	77.0069	384.217	.629	.904
CETSCALE3	76.1944	378.871	.159	.948
CETSCALE4	77.0000	379.958	.694	.902
CETSCALE5	78.1944	367.277	.741	.900
CETSCALE6	77.7292	369.108	.767	.899
CETSCALE7	77.5764	363.812	.797	.898
CETSCALE8	77.2847	377.897	.716	.902
CETSCALE9	77.2361	379.650	.754	.901
CETSCALE10	77.2500	381.895	.708	.902
CETSCALE11	77.8194	370.359	.747	.900
CETSCALE12	77.8125	381.888	.690	.903
CETSCALE13	77.0764	387.148	.646	.904
CETSCALE14	78.2222	375.629	.675	.902
CETSCALE115	77.6250	376.544	.704	.902
CETSCALE16	77.1528	390.382	.550	.906
CETSCALE17	77.6111	374.030	.714	.901

Scale Statistics

Mean	Variance	Std. Deviation	N of Items
82.2292	424.556	20.60474	17

As it is shown Cronbach Alpha is 0.910. So, reliability is good (0.910 > 0.7).

Next, the factor analysis is done as follows.

Analyze ⇨ Dimension Reduction ⇨ Factor

Related items are moved to right side (variables).Then, click on **descriptive** button and select the **Kmo and Barttlets test of Sphericity.**

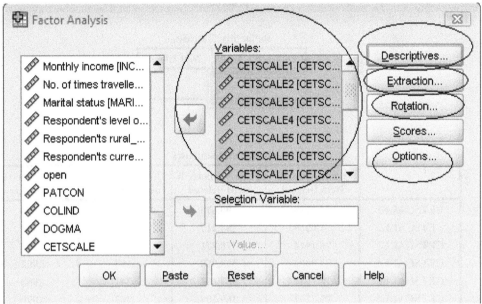

Figure 89

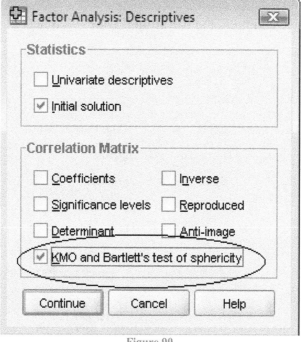

Figure 90

Then, click on continue and click on **extraction** button. In extraction, **method** should be adjusted in **principal components**.

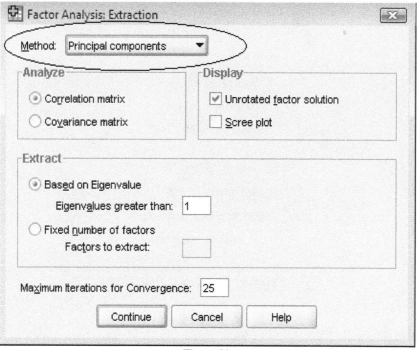

Figure 91

Next, click on continue and press the **Rotation** (Figure 89). Select the Varimax and continue.

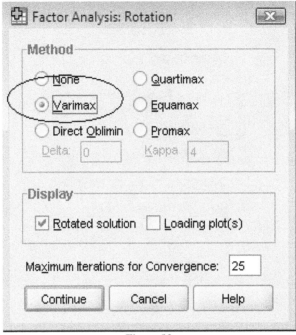

Figure 92

Then , click on **options** (Figure 89) and select **sorted by size** and continue.

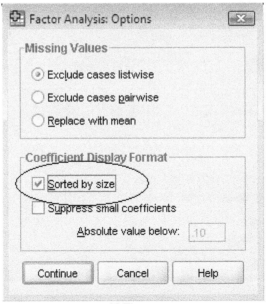

93 Figure

Finally , press the ok and get the out put.

Factor Analysis

KMO and Bartlett's Test

Kaiser-Meyer-Olkin Measure of Sampling Adequacy.		.929
Bartlett's Test of Sphericity	Approx. Chi-Square	1658.010
	df	136
	Sig.	.000

Communalities

	Initial	Extraction
CETSCALE1	1.000	.690
CETSCALE2	1.000	.720
CETSCALE3	1.000	.206
CETSCALE4	1.000	.681
CETSCALE5	1.000	.672
CETSCALE6	1.000	.697
CETSCALE7	1.000	.714
CETSCALE8	1.000	.599
CETSCALE9	1.000	.659
CETSCALE10	1.000	.614
CETSCALE11	1.000	.752
CETSCALE12	1.000	.608
CETSCALE13	1.000	.518
CETSCALE14	1.000	.705
CETSCALE115	1.000	.644
CETSCALE16	1.000	.383
CETSCALE17	1.000	.624

Extraction Method: Principal Component Analysis.

Total Variance Explained

Comp onent	Initial Eigenvalues			Extraction Sums of Squared Loadings			Rotation Sums of Squared Loadings		
	Total	% of Variance	Cumulative %	Total	% of Variance	Cumulative %	Total	% of Variance	Cumulative %
1	9.070	53.351	53.351	9.070	53.351	53.351	7.163	42.136	42.136
2	1.416	8.328	61.679	1.416	8.328	61.679	3.322	19.543	61.679
3	.986	5.802	67.481						
4	.906	5.331	72.812						

5	.678	3.987	76.798
6	.537	3.162	79.960
7	.490	2.880	82.839
8	.430	2.527	85.366
9	.398	2.342	87.709
10	.369	2.171	89.880
11	.347	2.043	91.923
12	.310	1.824	93.747
13	.301	1.772	95.519
14	.227	1.337	96.856
15	.202	1.186	98.042
16	.175	1.030	99.072
17	.158	.928	100.000

Extraction Method: Principal Component Analysis.

Component Matrix[a]

	Component	
	1	2
CETSCALE7	.843	-.065
CETSCALE6	.817	-.171
CETSCALE11	.815	-.297
CETSCALE9	.803	.119
CETSCALE5	.801	-.175
CETSCALE17	.776	-.146
CETSCALE10	.770	.144
CETSCALE8	.761	.142
CETSCALE115	.759	-.262
CETSCALE14	.745	-.388
CETSCALE4	.744	.358
CETSCALE12	.742	-.240
CETSCALE13	.718	-.043
CETSCALE2	.659	.534
CETSCALE16	.616	.057
CETSCALE1	.611	.563
CETSCALE3	.178	.418

Extraction Method: Principal Component Analysis.

a. 2 components extracted.

Rotated Component Matrix[a]		
	Component	
	1	2
CETSCALE11	.854	.149
CETSCALE14	.839	.036
CETSCALE6	.793	.259
CETSCALE115	.788	.152
CETSCALE5	.781	.248
CETSCALE12	.763	.162
CETSCALE7	.763	.364
CETSCALE17	.745	.261
CETSCALE13	.644	.321
CETSCALE9	.636	.504
CETSCALE10	.595	.510
CETSCALE8	.589	.503
CETSCALE16	.505	.357
CETSCALE1	.248	.793
CETSCALE2	.305	.792
CETSCALE4	.466	.681
CETSCALE3	-.055	.451

Extraction Method: Principal Component Analysis.
Rotation Method: Varimax with Kaiser Normalization.

a.   Rotation converged in 3 iterations.

Component Transformation Matrix

Component	1	2
1	.867	.499
2	-.499	.867

Extraction Method: Principal Component Analysis.
Rotation Method: Varimax with Kaiser Normalization.

Table of table of KMO and Bartlett's Test

In table of KMO and Bartlett's Test:
-If KMO measure of sampling adequacy index ≥ 0.8 , then the data can be used for EFA.In our case it is 0.929.

-If p-value was less than 0.05, then the data can be used for EFA. In our case it is 0.00.

*NOTICE: For identifying dimensions (factors) and the items under those dimensions (factors) use **rotated component matrix** table.

- Values in the rotated component matrix denote factor loadings.

-In rotated component matrix table the biggest number shows the belonging of its item to related component (Factor).

-For each item identify the factor loading that is maximum. The item is considered to be long to the factor where the factor loading is maximum.

-The maximum factor loading should not be less than 0.5.If any item has a maximum factor loading of less than 0.5, throw the item away from further analysis.

-In table only the items which their value is more than 0.5 are kept.

After throwing away of items which their value is less than 0.5 with in both factors, the table comes like as follows.

Factor 1	Factor 2
CETSCALE 11	CETSCALE 1
CETSCALE 14	CETSCALE 2
CETSCALE 6	CETSCALE 4
CETSCALE 15	
CETSCALE 5	
CETSCALE 12	
CETSCALE 7	
CETSCALE 17	
CETSCALE 13	
CETSCALE 9	
CETSCALE 10	
CETSCALE 8	
CETSCALE 16	

We threw a way CETSCALE 3 .Since , in both factors its value is below 0.5.

*NOTICE:In some books amount of factor loading is considered less than 0.3.However , in most of the authentic books its amount is less than 0.5.

Then , the process below is done.

Analyze ⇨ Dimension Reduction ⇨ Factor

All the previous process is done again. However, in **options** in addition of **sorted by size**, **suppress small coefficients** is selected and **absolute value below** is adjusted in 0.5.With adjusting the absolute value below on 0.5 , the values below 0.5 will be ignored and cleaned automatically.

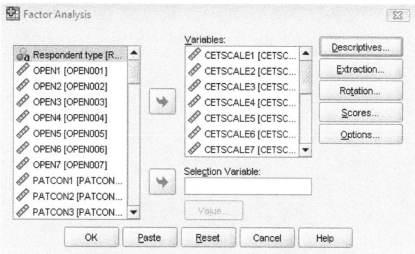

Figure 94

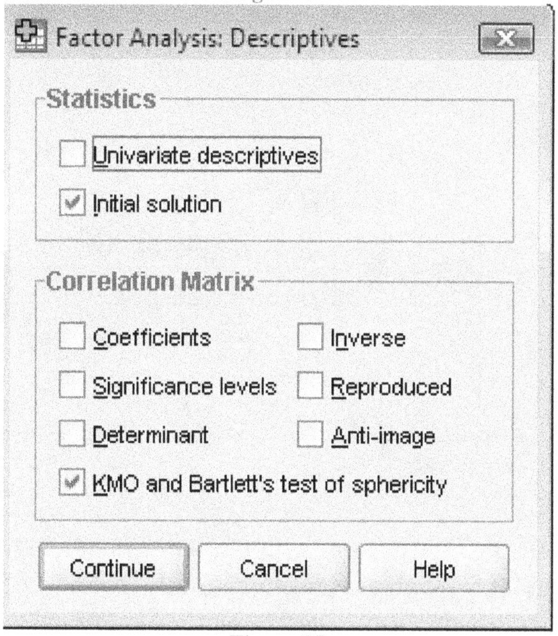

Figure 95

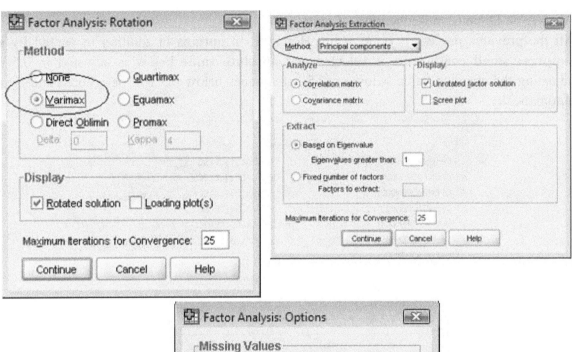

Figure 96

Next , press the continue and ok button.In the newly got **Rotated Component Matrix** table items with value less than 0.5 are cleaned automatically and no need to do that manually. For further analysis of factors the Summated Scale or Mean Scale is done.For example:

Factor 2
CETSCALE 1
CETSCALE 2
CETSCALE 4

For extra explanation regarding factor 2:
- The values of three CETSCALES above can be cumulated ➜ Summated scale
- The mean of CETSCALES can be calculated ➜ Mean Scale

For calculating Summated scale follow the below process.

Transform ⇨ Compute ⇨ variable

Create CETSCALE2 and move the CETSCALE 1 And CETSCALE 2 and CETSCALE 4 to right side and cumulate all together.

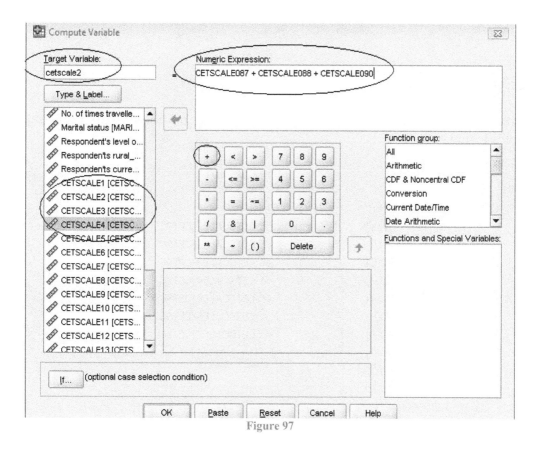

Figure 97

Then , click on ok button.As it is seen cetscale2 is added to our variables.

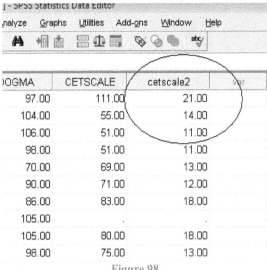

Figure 98

Next ,follow below process.

Analyze ⇨ Dimension Reduction ⇨ Factor ⇨ Click on Score Button and select Save as variables(Figure 99 & 100).

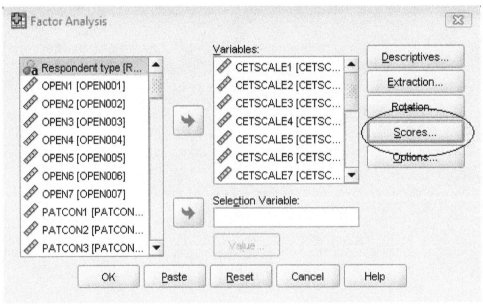

Figure 99

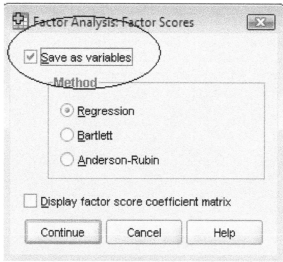

Figure 100

Press continue and ok.

If go back to **variable view**, two newly added variables can be observed as well as in data view two new variables are added.

	Name	Type	Width	Decimals	Label	Values	
72	CETSCALE...	Numeric	8	2	CETSCALE11	{1.00, Stron...	Noı
73	CETSCALE...	Numeric	8	2	CETSCALE12	{1.00, Stron...	Noı
74	CETSCALE...	Numeric	8	2	CETSCALE13	{1.00, Stron...	Noı
75	CETSCALE...	Numeric	8	2	CETSCALE14	{1.00, Stron...	Noı
76	CETSCALE...	Numeric	8	2	CETSCALE115	{1.00, Stron...	Noı
77	CETSCALE...	Numeric	8	2	CETSCALE16	{1.00, Stron...	Noı
78	CETSCALE...	Numeric	8	2	CETSCALE17	{1.00, Stron...	Noı
79	open	Numeric	8	2		None	Noı
80	PATCON	Numeric	8	2		None	Noı
81	COLIND	Numeric	8	2		None	Noı
82	DOGMA	Numeric	8	2		None	Noı
83	CETSCALE	Numeric	8	2		None	Noı
84	cetscale2	Numeric	8	2		None	Noı
85	FAC1_1	Numeric	11	5	REGR factor score 1 for analysis 1	None	Noı
86	FAC2_1	Numeric	11	5	REGR factor score 2 for analysis 1	None	Noı
87							
88							

Figure 101

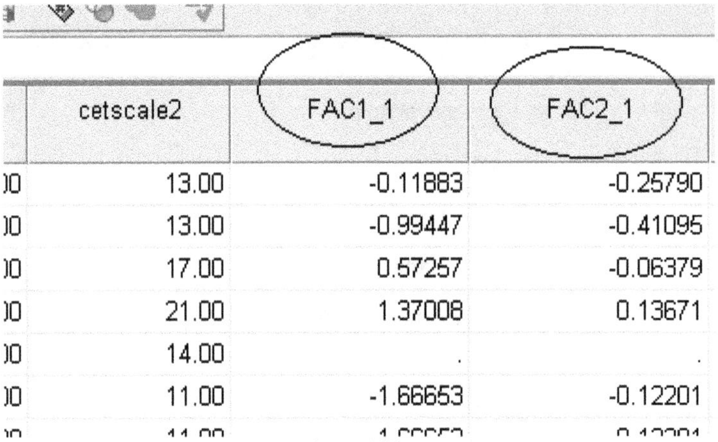

	cetscale2	FAC1_1	FAC2_1
)0	13.00	-0.11883	-0.25790
)0	13.00	-0.99447	-0.41095
)0	17.00	0.57257	-0.06379
)0	21.00	1.37008	0.13671
)0	14.00		.
)0	11.00	-1.66653	-0.12201
)0	11.00	1.66653	0.12201

Figure 102

Chapter 19: Nonparametric Test

What was written in previous chapters was related to parametric test.It means it was done under normality assumption conditions.However,When the normality assumption is not satisfied or when the sample size is small , we are involved with non parametric test.(Refer to defenitions in chapter one)

Parametric Test	Non Parametric test
One sample Test	Rank-Sum test
Independent sample Test	Mann-Whitney U Test
Anova	Kroskal wallis Test
Pearson Correlation	Spearman Correlation

Example1-19:

Refer to example two from chapter 11
First in **variable view** two variables EI ansd GENDER are described.Two values are given for gender.

Female= f=1
Male= m=2

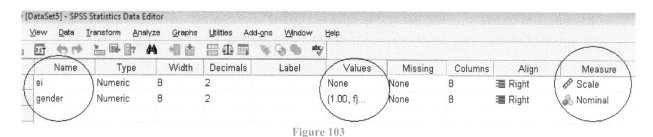

Figure 103

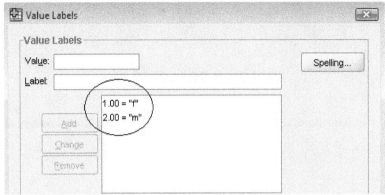

Figure 104

Then , data is entered.

	ei	gender
1	88.00	1.00
2	106.00	1.00
3	95.00	1.00
4	118.00	1.00
5	102.00	1.00
6	120.00	1.00
22	100.00	2.00
23	93.00	2.00
24	103.00	2.00
25	83.00	2.00
26		

Figure 105

Then , follow the procedure below.

Analyze ⇨ Nonparametric Test ⇨ 2 independent samples

EI is moved to test variable list and gender is shifted to grouping variable.Next , click on define groups button and enter number one for group 1 and number two for group2.

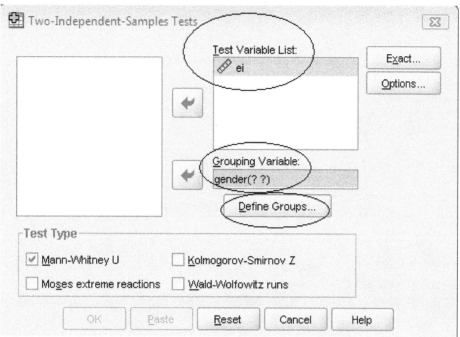

Figure 106

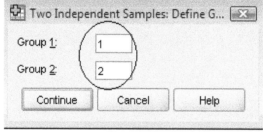

Figure 107

Click on continue and ok and get output.

Mann-Whitney Test

Ranks

	gender	N	Mean Rank	Sum of Ranks
ei	f	15	13.33	200.00
	m	10	12.50	125.00
	Total	25		

Test Statistics[b]

	ei
Mann-Whitney U	70.000
Wilcoxon W	125.000
Z	-.278
Asymp. Sig. (2-tailed)	.781
Exact Sig. [2*(1-tailed Sig.)]	.807[a]

a. Not corrected for ties.

b. Grouping Variable: gender

Report:

H0: EI female = EI male

H1: EI female ≠ EI male

We tested the above hypothesis using non-parametric test. We used non –parametric test. This is because , the data violated normality assumption .Based on the Mann-Whitney U test results(Mann-Whitney U =70.0, Z value = -0.278 , P-value = 0.807).p-value > 0.05.We find that the EI values of male and female are not significantly different.

Bibliography

18. Agresti, F. (2009). In *Statistical Methods for Social Sciences* (p. 136). pearson Education.

19. Brown, T. A. (2006). *Confirmatory factor analysis for applied research.* New York: Guilford.

20. Campell, D. T. (1959). Psychological Bulletin. *Convergent and discriminant validation by the multitrait-multimethod matrix* , 81-105.

13. Castillo, J. J. (2009). *STEPS OF THE SCIENTIFIC METHOD.* Retrieved from Experiment-Resources: www.experiment-resources.com/convenience-sampling.html,www.experiment-resources.com/judgmental-sampling.html,http://www.experiment-resources.com/snowball-sampling.html

5.Dean, S. (2010, february). *Descriptive Statistics: Skewness and the Mean, Median, and Mode.* Retrieved from connexions: http://cnx.org/content/m17104/latest/

25. Fisher R.A. (1926). The arrangement of field experiments. *Journal of the ministry of agriculture,vol 33* , 504.

1.Glenn D. Israel, a. p. (2009). Determining Sample Size. *Document is PEOD6, one of a series of the Agricultural Education and Communication Department, Florida Cooperative Extension Service* .

17. Greene, W. H. (2003). *Econometric Analysis (5th ed.).* Prentice Hall.

24. Hogg, R.V, Tanis, E.A, Probability and Statistical Inference,5th edition (p. 352).

10. Institute, S. (2006). *SAS Elementary Statistics Procedures.* Retrieved from SAS Institute: http://support.sas.com/onlinedoc/913/getDoc/en/proc.hlp/a002473332.htm

27. Norman L. Johnson and Samuel Kotz. (1970). *Continuous univariate distributions,chapter 13.* John Wiley & Sons.

8.Likert, R. (1932). A Technique for the Measurement of Attitudes. *Archives of Psychology 140* , 1–55.

22. Matthew Hesson-McInnis, P. (n.d.). *SPSS Basic Skills Tutorials.* Retrieved from Illinois State University: http://my.ilstu.edu/~mshesso/SPSS/tutorial.html

16.Probability Distribution. (2010). Retrieved from Investopedia: http://www.investopedia.com/terms/p/probabilitydistribution.asp

2.ROBERT V. KREJCIE University of Minnesota, D. &. (1970). DETERMINING SAMPLE SIZE FOR RESEARCH ACTIVITIES. *EDUCATIONAL AND PSYCHOLOGICAL MEASUREMENT* , 607-610.

23. Bernard A. Rosner. (2006). Fundamentals of biostatistics,Volume 1. Thomson Learning Academic Resource Center.

26.(2008). In P. A. Sarah Boslaugh, *Statistics in a nutshell* (p. 137).

21. Shepard, J., & Greene, R. W. (2003). *Shepard, Jon; Robert W. Greene.* Ohio: Glencoe: McGraw-Hill.

Skewness. (2010). Retrieved from Investopedia: www.investopedia.com/terms/s/skewness.asp

14.Statistical Glossary. (2004-2010). Retrieved from statistics.com: http://www2.statistics.com/resources/glossary/s/smplframe.php

22. Sullivan, A., & Sheffrin, S. M. (2003). In *Economics: Principles in action* (p. p. 334.). Upper Saddle River, New Jersey: Pearson Prentice Hall.

11. Trek, S. (2011). *Statistics Tutorial.* Retrieved from Stat Trek: http://stattrek.com/Lesson3/SamplingTheory.aspx

9.Trochim, Wiliam. M. (version current as october 20 ,2006). *Levels of Measurement.* Retrieved from Research Methods Knowledge Base: www.socialresearchmethods.net/kb/measlevl.php

15.Tutorials. (2008). Retrieved from emathzone: www.emathzone.com/tutorials/basic-statistics/sample-design-and-sampling-frame.htm

12. Neville H and Sidney T. (2004, January 6). *Discuss Sampling Methods.* Retrieved from Coventry University UK:
www.coventry.ac.uk/ec/~nhunt/meths/system.html,www.coventry.ac.uk/ec/~nhunt/meths/strati.html,www.coventry.ac.uk/ec/~nhunt/meths/cluster.html

4.Von Hippel, P. T. (2005). Mean, Median, and Skew: Correcting a Textbook Rule. *Journal of Statistics Education* , 13.

3. William Navidi, *Statistics for Engineers and Scientists* (2006), McGraw-Hill, pg 14

7.Wuensch, K. L. (2005, October 4). *What is a Likert Scale? and How Do You Pronounce 'Likert?* Retrieved from East California University: http://core.ecu.edu/psyc/wuenschk/StatHelp/Likert.htm.

"Cartoons which are used during the chapters, were sourced from Virtual Institute of Applied Science(VIAS.ORG)"

(1998-G.Meixner)

"Pictures which are used for designing the cover, were sourced from www.stockphotopro.com"

Appendix

Table 1. Sample size for ±3%, ±5%, ±7% and ±10% Precision Levels Where Confidence Level is 95% and P=.5.				
Size of	Sample Size (n) for Precision (e) of:			
Population	±3%	±5%	±7%	±10%
500	a	222	145	83
600	a	240	152	86
700	a	255	158	88
800	a	267	163	89
900	a	277	166	90
1,000	a	286	169	91
2,000	714	333	185	95
3,000	811	353	191	97
4,000	870	364	194	98
5,000	909	370	196	98
6,000	938	375	197	98
7,000	959	378	198	99
8,000	976	381	199	99
9,000	989	383	200	99
10,000	1,000	385	200	99
15,000	1,034	390	201	99
20,000	1,053	392	204	100
25,000	1,064	394	204	100
50,000	1,087	397	204	100
100,000	1,099	398	204	100
>100,000	1,111	400	204	100
a = Assumption of normal population is poor (Yamane, 1967). The entire population should be sampled.				

Table 1

Glenn D. Israel, Department of Agricultural Education and Communication, University of Florida, Determining Sample Size[1]

Table 2. Sample size for ±5%, ±7% and ±10% Precision Levels Where Confidence Level is 95% and P=.5.			
Size of	Sample Size (n) for Precision (e) of:		
Population	±5%	±7%	±10%
100	81	67	51
125	96	78	56
150	110	86	61
175	122	94	64
200	134	101	67
225	144	107	70
250	154	112	72
275	163	117	74
300	172	121	76
325	180	125	77
350	187	129	78
375	194	132	80
400	201	135	81
425	207	138	82
450	212	140	82

Table 2

Glenn D. Israel, Department of Agricultural Education and Communication, University of Florida, "Determining Sample Size",[1].

TABLE FOR DETERMINING SAMPLE SIZE FROM A GIVEN POPULATION

N	S	N	S	N	S	N	S	N	S
10	10	100	80	280	162	800	260	2800	338
15	14	110	86	290	165	850	265	3000	341
20	19	120	92	300	169	900	269	3500	246
25	24	130	97	320	175	950	274	4000	351
30	28	140	103	340	181	1000	278	4500	351
35	32	150	108	360	186	1100	285	5000	357
40	36	160	113	380	181	1200	291	6000	361
45	40	180	118	400	196	1300	297	7000	364
50	44	190	123	420	201	1400	302	8000	367
55	48	200	127	440	205	1500	306	9000	368
60	52	210	132	460	210	1600	310	10000	373
65	56	220	136	480	214	1700	313	15000	375
70	59	230	140	500	217	1800	317	20000	377
75	63	240	144	550	225	1900	320	30000	379
80	66	250	148	600	234	2000	322	40000	380
85	70	260	152	650	242	2200	327	50000	381
90	73	270	155	700	248	2400	331	75000	382
95	76	270	159	750	256	2600	335	100000	384

Table3

Note: "N" is population size
"S" is sample size.

Krejcie, Robert V., Morgan, Daryle W., "Determining Sample Size for Research Activities", Educational and Psychological Measurement, 1970. [2].

Normal Table — Areas of the Standard Normal Distribution

The entries in this table are the probabilities that a random variable with a standard normal distribution assumes a value between 0 and z; the probability is represented by the shaded area under the curve in the accompanying figure. Areas for negative values of z are obtained by symmetry.

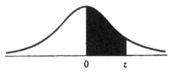

	Second Decimal Place in z									
z	0.00	0.01	0.02	0.03	0.04	0.05	0.06	0.07	0.08	0.09
0.0	0.0000	0.0040	0.0080	0.0120	0.0160	0.0199	0.0239	0.0279	0.0319	0.0359
0.1	0.0398	0.0438	0.0478	0.0517	0.0557	0.0596	0.0636	0.0675	0.0714	0.0753
0.2	0.0793	0.0832	0.0871	0.0910	0.0948	0.0987	0.1026	0.1064	0.1103	0.1141
0.3	0.1179	0.1217	0.1255	0.1293	0.1331	0.1368	0.1406	0.1443	0.1480	0.1517
0.4	0.1554	0.1591	0.1628	0.1664	0.1700	0.1736	0.1772	0.1808	0.1844	0.1879
0.5	0.1915	0.1950	0.1985	0.2019	0.2054	0.2088	0.2123	0.2157	0.2190	0.2224
0.6	0.2257	0.2291	0.2324	0.2357	0.2389	0.2422	0.2454	0.2486	0.2517	0.2549
0.7	0.2580	0.2611	0.2642	0.2673	0.2704	0.2734	0.2764	0.2794	0.2823	0.2852
0.8	0.2881	0.2910	0.2939	0.2967	0.2995	0.3023	0.3051	0.3078	0.3106	0.3133
0.9	0.3159	0.3186	0.3212	0.3238	0.3264	0.3289	0.3315	0.3340	0.3365	0.3389
1.0	0.3413	0.3438	0.3461	0.3485	0.3508	0.3531	0.3554	0.3577	0.3599	0.3621
1.1	0.3643	0.3665	0.3686	0.3708	0.3729	0.3749	0.3770	0.3790	0.3810	0.3830
1.2	0.3849	0.3869	0.3888	0.3907	0.3925	0.3944	0.3962	0.3980	0.3997	0.4015
1.3	0.4032	0.4049	0.4066	0.4082	0.4099	0.4115	0.4131	0.4147	0.4162	0.4177
1.4	0.4192	0.4207	0.4222	0.4236	0.4251	0.4265	0.4279	0.4292	0.4306	0.4319
1.5	0.4332	0.4345	0.4357	0.4370	0.4382	0.4394	0.4406	0.4418	0.4429	0.4441
1.6	0.4452	0.4463	0.4474	0.4484	0.4495	0.4505	0.4515	0.4525	0.4535	0.4545
1.7	0.4554	0.4564	0.4573	0.4582	0.4591	0.4599	0.4608	0.4616	0.4625	0.4633
1.8	0.4641	0.4649	0.4656	0.4664	0.4671	0.4678	0.4686	0.4693	0.4699	0.4706
1.9	0.4713	0.4719	0.4726	0.4732	0.4738	0.4744	0.4750	0.4756	0.4761	0.4767
2.0	0.4772	0.4778	0.4783	0.4788	0.4793	0.4798	0.4803	0.4808	0.4812	0.4817
2.1	0.4821	0.4826	0.4830	0.4834	0.4838	0.4842	0.4846	0.4850	0.4854	0.4857
2.2	0.4861	0.4864	0.4868	0.4871	0.4875	0.4878	0.4881	0.4884	0.4887	0.4890
2.3	0.4893	0.4896	0.4898	0.4901	0.4904	0.4906	0.4909	0.4911	0.4913	0.4916
2.4	0.4918	0.4920	0.4922	0.4925	0.4927	0.4929	0.4931	0.4932	0.4934	0.4936
2.5	0.4938	0.4940	0.4941	0.4943	0.4945	0.4946	0.4948	0.4949	0.4951	0.4952
2.6	0.4953	0.4955	0.4956	0.4957	0.4959	0.4960	0.4961	0.4962	0.4963	0.4964
2.7	0.4965	0.4966	0.4967	0.4968	0.4969	0.4970	0.4971	0.4972	0.4973	0.4974
2.8	0.4974	0.4975	0.4976	0.4977	0.4977	0.4978	0.4979	0.4979	0.4980	0.4981
2.9	0.4981	0.4982	0.4982	0.4983	0.4984	0.4984	0.4985	0.4985	0.4986	0.4986
3.0	0.4987	0.4987	0.4987	0.4988	0.4988	0.4989	0.4989	0.4989	0.4990	0.4990
3.1	0.4990	0.4991	0.4991	0.4991	0.4992	0.4992	0.4992	0.4992	0.4993	0.4993
3.2	0.4993	0.4993	0.4994	0.4994	0.4994	0.4994	0.4994	0.4995	0.4995	0.4995
3.3	0.4995	0.4995	0.4995	0.4996	0.4996	0.4996	0.4996	0.4996	0.4996	0.4997
3.4	0.4997	0.4997	0.4997	0.4997	0.4997	0.4997	0.4997	0.4997	0.4997	0.4998
3.5	0.4998	0.4998	0.4998	0.4998	0.4998	0.4998	0.4998	0.4998	0.4998	0.4998
3.6	0.4998	0.4998	0.4999	0.4999	0.4999	0.4999	0.4999	0.4999	0.4999	0.4999
3.7	0.4999									
4.0	0.49997									
4.5	0.499997									
5.0	0.4999997									

Table 4

ABOUT THE AUTHOR

This is author's first book and he finished it at the end of 2010.Seyed Reza Hashemian Rahaghi currently is taking his Master of Science with specialization in Finance in UPM University which is located in Malaysia. He got his bachelor in Business Administration and Associate Degree in Biomedical Science from University of Urmia and Islamic Azad University in Iran respectively. He has 6 years work experience in health related organizations and official parts.

www.ingramcontent.com/pod-product-compliance
Lightning Source LLC
Chambersburg PA
CBHW080411060326
40689CB00019B/4206